Praise

Profound Insights

Debora McLaughlin knows what it takes for women to step up to their greatness by finding their inner balance and grounding their roots of genius each time they step into their high heels! Humor, grace, and profound insight are only some of the gifts you will enjoy in *Running in High Heels.*

Susan Hayward, Energy and Feng Shui Master

Engaging Storytelling

In today's increasingly complex world of work, we need the leadership attributes and change intelligence women possess to find powerful solutions to the challenges we face. *Running in High Heels* gives you the strategies you need to leverage your success while standing tall in your heels. The case studies are powerful and Debora's storytelling engaging with a renegade edge.

Barbara A. Trautlein, PhD, Best-Selling Author of *Change Intelligence: Use the Power of CQ to Lead, Change that Sticks* and Principal of Change Catalysts, LLC

A New Consciousness

Leadership is all about relationships. *Running in High Heels* celebrates the unique relationship women can have with self, through leading others and by serving as the leader of an organization. All empower you to manifest your best relationship, changing your personal and professional paradigms from the current norm of "the survival of the fittest" to a Power of We mindset, which is fundamental to the emerging new consciousness.

Beth Banning, Best-Selling Author and CEO of Your Thriving Business

Discover Your Voice

Running in High Heels keeps you laughing and motivated while discovering what leadership shoes are right for you. For your message to be heard, personally and professionally, you need to discover your voice, project it, and attract attention to it with your beautiful tone. *Running in High Heels* sings the song for women worldwide.

Orgena Rose, Voice Expert, Singer, Dancer, Actor

Get Noticed

Executives need more than ever to distinguish themselves in their industry. *Running in High Heels* encourages you to bring out your own celebrity and to control your brand before one is established for you. *Running in High Heels* will get you noticed.

Ruth Klein, Expert, Celebrity Branding

Activate Your Full Potential

Reveal your truth. Connect with your unique genius. Stand in your power, no matter what shoes you wear. *Running in High Heels* will uproot any beliefs that hold you back and help you to discover the well of confidence and determination you possess. Offering tips from top women CEOs, *Running in High Heels* will connect the dots of your life story and enable you to see its fullest potential so you can design the life and career you desire.

Laurie Rubinstein, CEO, Step into Great

An Array of Resources

Today's leaders need to inspire excellence in themselves, their teams, and the organization. To be a leader in today's changing business climate, you need access to the resources to support you. *Running in High Heels* offers a vast array of resources to access your authentic leadership and unleash your feminine side, to build trust and engagement in your teams.

Quenby Rubin-Sprague M.H.R.O.D., RD

Build Your Brand Image

Running in High Heels is about showing your power as a woman so you are seen, heard, and noticed. Building an image informs others of your ability to influence and at the same time makes a memorable impression that creates opportunism for you. Stand out by building your image.

Vaska Krabbe, Image Expert

A Tool Kit in a Book

There has never been a more exciting time for women in business to get as far ahead as we desire. And to carve out or create careers and jobs that speak to who we really are. However, we need to be clear about what we bring to the table, what we want, *and* we need to know how to bend the rules of the game to suit our unique personality, strengths, and goals. Debora is an expert at doing "corporate" in a truly empowering way that makes you thrive and allows you to be fully yourself (as opposed to just coping and trying to fit in). Make the most of this special time and dig in to her tool kit of book!

Rikke Hansen, CEO, Career on Your Terms

Takes You on a Journey to Discover Your Authentic Self

Every leader and organization needs to tell their brand story, creating the know, like, and trust factor. *Running in High Heels* takes you on a journey to reveal your authentic self and to discover what you truly are capable of.

Michelle Lange, CEO, M Lange Media

Accelerate Your Success

With its savvy advice, *Running in High Heels* will give you an advantage to accelerate your success!

Sybil Henry, The Style Concierge, Author of
Style Yourself, Over 40, 50 and Beyond

Executive-Level Power Strategies

Every executive needs to navigate the road of leadership: Bridging the gap between employees, stakeholders, and consumers isn't an easy job; it takes agility and flexibility. *Running in High Heels* gives you executive-level power strategies to lead yourself, your team, and your organization without breaking a heel.

Karen Bill, Executive Director

Also Authored by Debora J. McLaughlin

The Renegade Leader: 9 Success Strategies Driven Leaders Use to Ignite People, Ignite Performance & Profits

Blueprint for Business Success

Co-Authored Titles by Debora J. McLaughlin

No Winner Ever Got There Without a Coach with David Rock, et al.

Straight Talk on Getting Results: Corporate America's 10 Most Requested Speakers and Trainers with Mona Pearl, et al.

Roadmap for Career Success with Lisa Martelli

Blueprint for Success: Proven Strategies for Success and Survival with Ken Blanchard, Stephen R. Covey, et al.

RUNNING IN
High Heels

HOW TO LEAD WITH
INFLUENCE, IMPACT & INGENUITY

DEBORA J. MCLAUGHLIN

BALBOA.
PRESS
A DIVISION OF HAY HOUSE

Author Credits: Amazon Best-Selling Author
Cover Design: Lauren Kudo
Photography: IStockPhoto
Editor: Lisa Canfield

Balboa Press books may be ordered through booksellers or by contacting:

Balboa Press
A Division of Hay House
1663 Liberty Drive
Bloomington, IN 47403
www.balboapress.com
1 (877) 407-4847

Printed in the United States of America.

ISBN: 978-1-4525-8821-6 (sc)
ISBN: 978-1-4525-8823-0 (hc)
ISBN: 978-1-4525-8822-3 (e)

Library of Congress Control Number: 2013922424

Balboa Press rev. date: 11/13/2014

To my mother Rosemary, who wore her Crocs but dreamed of her red high heels. Dedicated to those who choose to stand tall and make a difference in their life, in the lives of others, and in the world. Wear your shoes proudly and leave great heel prints behind.

CONTENTS

INTRODUCTION:
STEPPING INTO YOUR
POWER SHOE

I remember when I was first introduced to the shoes.

It was my first visit to New York City since a childhood trip with my father and sister. The day was hot—it was summer—and I could feel the heat rising from the pavement of the intersection where I sat in traffic.

I was 21, my bags were packed, and the moving truck was on its way. I was relocating to New York City to work for Digital Equipment Corporation.

That's when I noticed the shoes. At each intersection, a hive of professionals crossed the street. Oblivious to the traffic and the scenery around them, they all looked forward, determined to get to where they were going. The men dressed in suits and polished wing tips, the women in a variety of attire but with one commonality: They all wore sneakers. They needed to get to places fast so below their silk skirts, the well-woven fabrics of their suits, the refined lines of their linen pants, were sneakers of all colors and sizes.

I would soon learn about the shoes, the open-toed pumps, the brightly colored or rich black leather shoes that captured the small ray of sunshine between the tall buildings and reflected off them, the heels that were hidden in their bags and their briefcases, and hanging out of the side of their designer purses.

Within one week I became one of them, quickly scurrying down Wall Street to visit a prospective client and always pausing on the front steps, in the shadow of the building, to bend down and slip into my heels—the heels that would click across the marble foyer, present themselves to the security guards, elongate my 5-foot 3-inch body, and improve my posture in the elevator to the top floors where I would be with the decision-makers who dominated the executive suites.

Little did anyone know the fear I felt in the pit of my stomach as the elevator made its climb. I was a small-town girl from upper New York who suspected I would need more than product information and a smile to succeed. I worked for the largest vendor of computer systems and was on the cutting edge of technology. The decade brought the birth of Apple, AT&T, Microsoft Windows, and the first Hewlett-Packard microcomputers. It was my job to be the disrupter, to convince large organizations to uproot what they knew and go with the unknown.

Looking back I now see the value of the opportunity I had, to stand on the edge of innovation, bringing information technology to organizations that would change the very way they did business, reinvent how employees and customers interacted, and determine who succeeded in business.

Lining the sidewalks of Wall Street, my potential clients included Bankers Trust New York Corporation, the largest commercial bank in the United States and multibillion dollar bank holding company, Chase Manhattan, Citibank, and other top financial firms.

At that time I didn't know the culture or the language of big business. I didn't have the business experience I have now, and I sensed a handful of sales skills would not be enough to win the trust of those in the glass-walled boardrooms.

I had to shift my belief from fear and doubt to self-belief in what was possible. Like the technology solutions I was offering, I had to evolve and as result I succeeded.

Perhaps you remember a time when you faced a challenge but knew the only choice was to proceed. Most times moving forward is the key to success.

When I worked with top executives from Fortune 500 companies in New York City and Boston, I had to learn to slide into my own power shoes before entering the skyscrapers that overshadowed me. Now, with over 20 years' experience leveraging my own femininity and the natural attributes associated with it, I'm here to help you slide into yours.

Marilyn Monroe once said, "Give a girl the right shoes, and she can conquer the world."

And I believe that statement to be true.

Are you ready to step into your own power and own it? To, regardless of position, lead forward and discover how to embody leadership in yourself, in your teams, and within your organization? Imagine standing tall and powerfully in your intuitive self and feeling richly satisfied in all that you do.

Over my 20-plus year career in business, first as a top-performing sales executive and later as a coach to Fortune 500 executives, CEOs, and organizational leaders, I've learned that the shoes make all the difference. Especially for women leaders.

Slip into the right pair of shoes and they can take you all the way to the top.

And it doesn't matter if you're a Prada girl or prefer the comfort of flats. The heels I'm talking about are metaphorical more than literal— the kind of business savvy that turns heads in the same way stilettos do, attracting the admiration of others in your chosen field. Putting yourself at the highest elevation so you can be seen, heard, and noticed.

This book is for you if you want to break free of the status quo, turn your ideas into edgy, actionable leadership strategies, and stand out in today's modern economy while working more effectively, not harder. It offers the key strategies to navigate the ever-changing terrain of business.

And be comfortable in your own shoes.

It's about figuring out how to fit in with others without losing who you are or sacrificing your personal life. Discovering how to show up unapologetically as yourself to create an authentic and powerful leadership presence. Learning to effectively communicate your message so that it is heard, understood, and acted upon.

It's your time.

Because for the first time in business history, there are unprecedented opportunities for women at all levels to step up and take the lead.

Throughout these pages, you'll discover current research, live interviews with top women CEOs and case studies featuring some of my own clients—all designed to pull back the curtain and reveal the real-world strategies that will help you step into your greatness.

I'll serve as your personal executive leadership coach and guide through the hallways that lead to the executive suite—and beyond. I'll share strategies for success directly from women who have actively advanced to senior levels of leadership and the secrets of the women who lead some of the nation's largest companies. These trailblazers are in the best position to provide inside information on how to step over the obstacles encountered on the leadership runway and how to navigate around our self-made barriers to success.

We'll start with the basics of self-leadership, identifying your career trajectory and understanding which skills to use to leverage leadership. Next we move to clicking your heels with others, how to effectively manage a team and ignite the entrepreneurial spirit in others. Ultimately, we'll look at stepping into the big shoes of leading an organization, focusing how to lead with influence and impact and design your legacy—the heel prints you wish to leave behind.

Running in High Heels offers you the strides for success whether your track on the leadership runway includes owning the keys to biggest office, taking charge of your career for leadership advancement, or creating a high-performing team.

It will take you from where you are to where you want to be.

What you will learn from reading the case studies, from gaining insight from top women CEOs and the working feedback from women executives is this: Women are no longer looking to break the glass ceiling but are rewriting the rules instead of leaning into those designed by the males before them.

Women are creating their own authentic management style and taking renegade steps to get to the top in business, in career, and in life. You can do the same.

How to Get the Most from *Running in High Heels*

Business is evolving and its changes demand the attributes you bring to the table. It's my goal to point out your greatest assets and how to leverage them. Utilize the exercises suggested within each chapter, journal your responses to the questions at the end of each chapter, ponder the insights provided, and observe what happens when you truly step into your unique leadership. There is something for leaders of all levels along the way. As you read each chapter take time to pause in self-reflection. Visit http://www.therenegadeleader.com/BookResources for additional resources to support you along the way. Here you will find self-assessments, tip sheets and training resources to help you to maximize your leadership skills, gain influence and recognition and leverage your career while balancing work demands with your personal life.

Use what you learn to *Rethink* what it means to be a leader. Begin to *reimagine* what might be possible for you and your business, and think about ways in which you can *reinvent* your leadership, your team, or your organization to stay relevant.

Running in High Heels is centered on four stiletto strategies to leverage, engage, activate, and define leadership by using the L.E.A.D. Forward Formula™:

L is for Leverage: How to Lead with a Powerful Authentic Presence

E is for Engage: How to Motivate and Move People to Passion, Positivity, and Possibility

A is for Activate: How to Ignite a Culture of Collaboration and Innovation

D is for Distinguish: How to Distinguish Yourself and Your Organization

When you apply the L.E.A.D. Forward Formula™ you will:

- Project a seasoned, credible leadership presence.

- Gain visibility and recognition for your accomplishments.

- Build a reputation as a leader, expert, or go-to person.

- Navigate organizational politics with savvy.

- Create your sphere of influence.

- Leverage your network to gain access to hidden resources, information, and opportunities.

- Cultivate influence and get buy-in for ideas and initiatives.

- Be recognized as a leader others choose to follow.

Organizations can benefit from *Running in High Heels* by:

- Gaining an impactful leader who is seen, heard, and noticed, and who wins the hearts of her followers.

- Distinguishing your organization from its competitors and attracting top talent by valuing the contribution of women leaders.

- Powerfully engaging your high-potential leaders to be supported and valued.

- Creating a stronger leadership pipeline of women leaders in your organization.

- Giving women leaders what they need to successful navigate their career in leadership.

The leaders of many of the world's fastest-growing companies are in discussion about what business will look like in the future. The facts indicate what we have now is not working.

If the world is going to change for the better it will probably be related to the actions of business leaders.

As a woman in leadership you have an advantage you didn't have before. I wrote *Running in High Heels* because the time for women to take the lead and succeed is now.

So let's get started.

1 THE NEW PARADIGM OF LEADERSHIP - AND WHY WOMEN WILL LEAD THE WAY

When it comes to leadership, there's a whole new paradigm—and women are uniquely positioned to lead the way.

Why? Well, we know for starters that the old ways are no longer effective.

My clients ask: How can I:

- Lead change?

- Manage complexity?

- Prepare for emerging markets?

- Retain and develop top talent?

- Spur the entrepreneurial spirit of innovation?

- Change the way we work to be more productive?

- Gain more control and less chaos to minimize uncertainty?

Many leaders are struggling. They don't seem to be as effective anymore, or their people don't seem to be as responsive. Direct orders no longer go unquestioned, and few teams leave a conference room ready to leap into action.

Instead, people ask why, demand information, and seek answers before committing themselves to anything new. Everyone looks busy but not a lot of work is being done.

It's no secret today's leaders need to be able to successfully handle the uncertainly, the pace of change, and the amount of complexity that we face in our organizations.

We are hitting problems and challenges that we never experienced before. As a result, business performance is on the decline, employee motivation and engagement are at an all-time low, and businesses are wondering how they can grow with the people and resources they have.

Change is everywhere—not just in the workplace. Think of the technology you've added to your life: You carry thousands of songs in your pocket, your computer is as thin as your portfolio, a world of information is at your fingertips, and you have "friends" from around the world via social networking.

It really shouldn't come as a surprise that people have grown and changed as well. They have different needs than employees of the past.

Today's employees are smarter, more innovative, more creative, and full of potential. Many grew up with technology and thrive on a sense of community. Social contacts are just as important as family members, even more so for younger generations. Unlike team members from 10 or 20 years ago, today's workers like the feel of collaboration and want to be actively involved in decisions that affect their work.

But many of today's leaders, no matter how long they've been at it, are unsure of how to manage these 21st-century employees and organizations are unprepared for the Generation X and Y emerging leaders of tomorrow. "Management-centered" or "command-and-control" models of leadership have been proven to breed a lack of accountability and creativity, increased resentment, and poor outcomes.

Leaders are looking for answers, yet previously accepted models for success are proving to be vulnerable.

The bottom line is this: For business to succeed we need a seismic shift in how we lead.

Unfortunately business won't survive if we only look in the rear-view mirror to plan our future.

Since 1955 more than 90% of the companies on the Fortune 500 list have gone bankrupt, shrunk in size, become inconsequential, been mopped up by their rivals, or closed their doors. Sixty percent of CEOs think their current business model is only sustainable for another three years. Jim Collins's *Good to Great* was followed by *As the Mighty Fall,* noting how most of the "Good to Great" organizations closed their doors, shrunk in size, or were acquired by smaller competitors. Long-term strategic plans are permeable to the ever-changing business landscape.

If leaders are not on their toes, smaller, more agile companies will sprint by. Robert Safian of *Fast Company* coined the term "Generation Flux" to explain how the dizzying velocity of change in our economy has made chaos the defining feature of modern business. New companies—even industries—rise and fall faster than ever. Witness Apple, Facebook, and Amazon; witness Research in Motion, Blockbuster, and MySpace.

Size no longer matters as the quicker and more agile younger entrepreneurial companies are gaining unprecedented wins from their larger established competitors. It's harder than ever to stay ahead of your competition.

So you might be left wondering what style of leadership *does* work and *will* get you the results you need. No wonder the keyword "leadership style" was searched on Google by hundreds of thousands of people this month alone.

Men and women alike are frustrated.

The truth is, with all the talk about what makes a great leader, it can seem like an elusive goal that you can only reach if you have that perfect combination of impact, engagement, and influence. If you achieve this, your big vision will become a reality, leading your company to great success.

But we all know it's not that easy. As an executive coach, I work with leaders who hate their jobs, feel their message isn't understood, and have unresponsive teams. Essentially, their vision isn't happening fast enough and may not happen at all.

The answer is this: You can't do things according to the status quo. We must create a new paradigm of forward-thinking leaders and savvy risk-takers who lead with innovation, impact, and ingenuity, and are willing to keep moving forward, even if they can't see far ahead.

I call these leaders Renegade Leaders.

I introduced Renegade Leadership in the book *The Renegade Leader: 9 Success Strategies Driven Leaders Use to Ignite People, Performance and Profits.*

I named my company The Renegade Leader Coaching and Consulting Group because a new paradigm of business is emerging and in order to succeed you need to be a Renegade.

It takes a different type of leader to navigate the new business terrain. You need the capacity to zig when others zag. And that's the secret of Renegade Leaders: Renegade Leaders begin as leaders and learn these attributes along the way.

Renegade Leaders reimagine, rethink, and reinvent themselves and their companies in order to stay relevant. Renegade Leaders think in a groundbreaking way to attain goals. They value innovation and develop an ability to take risks and test new ideas. It's this entrepreneurial approach that becomes their competitive advantage. They can engineer projects from conception to delivery with an energy and drive to quickly implement new ideas, leaving behind every compromise.

Renegade Leaders have a long-term vision for their company that involves playing big, making no excuses, and staying fiercely dedicated to their company's growth. As front-runners, they are the first to implement new ideas and innovations. They see possibility where others see barriers. Renegade Leaders are creative, flexible, and current. Failure is not an option. Despite anxiety, fear, and the opinions of others, Renegade Leaders take strategic risks and make their big visions happen.

You're a Renegade, too.

Just by virtue of being a woman in business, you're a Renegade Leader. You've already had to juggle it all, break through barriers and remain standing and now you can show the world of business what you are capable of.

RENEGADES IN HEELS: WHY WOMEN ARE THE PERFECT FIT

In 2009 the Dalai Lama took people by surprise by proclaiming that Western women will save the world. Could it be true?

Extensive research has shown that there's a largely untapped resource out there that has exactly what it takes to transform the modern workplace.

A resource with the innate skills and talents necessary to engage with today's employees and bring out their very best.

A resource perfectly positioned to lead smart, savvy businesses to a new level of passion, productivity, and profit.

That resource is you.

The ideal management style for today's business climate is evolving. The traditional top-down hierarchical organizational structures, generally led by men, are changing to a collaborative team approach that emphasizes open communication, empathy, and employee inspiration and motivation.

Traits that come naturally to heel-wearers—and can be learned by men.

Not only that, studies are now proving that women confer greater corporate stability, profitability, and shareholder value.

We are in a global economy that yearns for a more right-brain, collaborative, solution-focused, more moderate thinking style and consensus-building communicators to create sustainable businesses.

For years, women have been told they need to change their fundamental nature—to communicate more aggressively, to reduce empathy and to lead by control. These recommendations are based on studies of leadership dating back decades. Not only that, these studies typically measure women's performance according to a traditionally male-oriented model of leadership, which is a model that no longer even works for men either.

Theorists argue that men and women differ in their leadership approaches. Women are classified as "transformational leaders," inspiring others through common goals and shared values. Men are "transactional leaders," focused on the tasks of leadership. Women take an interpersonal approach while men take a more management-oriented one. And in the past, this indicated that men were more effective leaders.

Men got things done. And this worked, until recently. Today they, too, are wondering how to lead more effectively in the modern economy. So now the question is not *How do women need to change to be more like men in the workplace?*, but *How do leaders, both men and women, flex to support the needs of today's workforce in order to create successful, sustainable businesses?*

When we take the 30,000-foot view of business, we can see that what the workforce demands is no longer a match to the leadership that is in place. At this point in history, women are more naturally inclined than men to produce a better outcome.

For the past decade I've been a constant study of leadership. I read all of the employee engagement studies. I've coached leaders of all levels, employees who were miserable at work, front-line managers who cried in the bathroom because their people wouldn't do what they wanted them to do, and CEOs who dreamed of growth but were held back by the performance of their workforce.

Success leaves clues. I am a success watcher, and I bring what I learn into my business and help my clients to do the same.

I knew a new model of leadership was needed and researched the companies that were moving forward with innovation and riding the turbulent economic waves with glee.

I started to notice patterns of those who succeeded in leadership and those who didn't. Those who did were able to influence performance results. They focused on people first and profits last; and had the skill set to build relationships, to listen to their workforce, to enroll others in their vision, and to create a culture of collaboration and creativity to gain the results they desired. I was able to systematize this process for my clients, teaching CEOs how to shift their culture to fit the modern economy and leaders how to adapt the skill set for today's workforce.

I started to bring these leadership tools to my clients and to their organizations. Breaking out from the norm and adopting a new paradigm of leadership—the Renegade model—became a new way of walking.

I knew my philosophy wouldn't be shared by all, that I would have to convince female leaders that they didn't have to wear the man's suit to fit in with the boys, and, in fact, they would succeed better without it. I also had to convince male leaders that if they opened their eyes to a softer, engaging, inclusive and transparent way of leading and motivating their employees, their profits would rise and they would achieve all they had envisioned.

It was a monumental task but I was willing to take it on. My gut wouldn't let it go. And then the proof started to come in.

My clients began increasing profits, surpassing those in their industries. Unlike many organizations that were shrinking or, worse, closing their doors, they opened new locations, hired employees, and even launched their own non-profits to generously share the wealth. In addition, they were regaining their lives, leaving the office in time to be home with their families, meeting deadlines without late-night sweats, and taking long-term vacations.

And their departments, organizations, and teams were still standing when they returned.

Not only were my clients gaining results from their new way of leading, researchers were starting to find proof that introducing this style, a more feminine style of leadership, had a positive effect on organizational leadership.

- The Zenger Folkman study compared 16 differentiating leadership competencies in men and women. Women not only outscored men in nurturing competencies like developing others and relationship building, we also outscored men in taking initiative, practicing self-development, integrity/honesty, and driving for results.

- In a study of 2,250 leaders, the PEW Center found that the women leaders in their report rated higher in areas of creativity, honesty, diligence, compassion, and empathy.

- The June 2013 *Inc. Magazine* cover story "Between Venus and Mars" lists the key attributes needed by effective leaders as empathy, vulnerability, humility, inclusiveness, generosity, balance, and patience—all traits once thought to be feminine.

And these are only the beginning.

> *"We're looking at a different paradigm of leadership, and it plays naturally to the strengths of women; the tide has turned. The leadership skills that come naturally to women are now absolutely necessary for companies to continue to thrive. It certainly is the reverse of how it was when I started out in the workplace. It seems like poetic justice."*
>
> ~ Regina Sacha, VP of HR, Federal Express

The fact is, there's never been a better time to be a woman in the business world. There have never been more opportunities for smart, talented women who want to lead. And you don't have to trade your Jimmy Choos for wing tips to do it. You can lead as an authentic, feminine leader.

We women, we're collaborative. We're consensus-builders.

We're great communicators. Women rate high on empathy, listening, and humility, and, as the majority of buyers are women, we are better connected with the needs of today's consumer.

These are the qualities that give us a unique advantage in the business world.

Past decades were about the "doing" of leadership and organizational development. Today's leader focuses on the "being" of leadership: being the leader others model, creating a culture of leadership, and being the leader who invigorates the highest performance in the individuals he/she oversees. Today's employees expect their leader to be more engaged, to be visible, to be transparent, and to walk their talk. To care about people.

Women, by nature, put people first.

Let's look in detail at the Zenger Folkman study.

The study conducted by Jack Zenger and Joseph Folkman researched 16 differentiating leadership competencies between men and women in the most successful and progressive organizations in the world:

- Takes initiative.

- Practices self-development.

- Displays high integrity and honesty.

- Drives for results.

- Develops others.

- Inspires and motivates others.

- Builds relationships.

- Collaborates.

- Establishes stretch goals.

- Champions change.

- Solves and analyzes issues.

- Communicates powerfully and prolifically.

- Connects the group to the outside world.

- Innovates.

- Possesses technical or professional expertise.

- Develops strategic perspective.

The study reported that women excelled in the majority of these areas.

Using a 360 assessment, women were rated by their peers, managers, and other associates as overall far better leaders than their male counterparts. The higher the level in position, the bigger the performance gap was. Zenger Folkman's research states: "Specifically, at all levels, women are rated higher in fully 12 of the 16 competencies that go into outstanding leadership. And two of the traits where women outscored men to the highest degree—taking initiative and driving for results—have long been thought of as particularly male strengths. As it happened, men outscored women significantly on only one management competence in this survey—the ability to develop a strategic perspective."

What Does This Mean for Women in the Workplace?

"The implications of this research are quite profound," Jack Zenger, CEO and co-founder of Zenger Folkman, stated. "It is a well-known fact that women are underrepresented at senior levels of management. Yet the data suggests that by adding more women, the overall effectiveness of the leadership team would go up."

Joe Folkman, president of Zenger Folkman, noted, "While men excel in the technical and strategic arenas, women clearly have the advantage in the extremely important areas of people relationships and communication. They also surpass their male counterparts in driving for results."

The MIT Center for Collective Intelligence (CCI) also pinpoints social perception ("the ability to sense what other people are thinking and feeling") as the key differentiator that results in high-performing teams and cultures. CCI founder Thomas Malone commented, "In business today, that skill is more prevalent among women."

The truth is these traits are needed for outstanding leadership, for both men and women.

What this means for you is this: Tap into your natural resources and you will succeed in leadership. Not only will you become the leader others choose to follow, but you will discover leading others is easier with collaboration, engagement, and creativity.

And the Zenger Folkman study was just one of many.

Think of the financial impact you can have. When businesses succeed we can give more. Women tend to create great work cultures, and to give back in their communities and to the world at large.

John Gerzema documents his study in *The Athena Doctrine*. A total of 64,000 people in 13 countries were asked their opinion about government, the economy, and the (mostly) male leaders leading the charge. The result? Two-thirds said the world would be a better place if "men thought more like women."

The Credit Suisse Research Institute recently found that companies with at least one woman at the table for their executive meetings outperformed in share prices when compared to companies that had no women at the helm. With today's economy, increased share prices are statistics that even the highest-performing male CEO cannot ignore.

The Haas School of Business at the University of California, Berkeley, reports that companies with more women on their boards perform better on environmental, social, and governance issues; and study after study supports that companies with gender-diverse boards outperform male bastions.

The evidence is in. Let's celebrate, jump up and down, and take out our party shoes. This is a big win for women. You are a match for what organizations need and what your people demand. You can stand tall in leadership.

Meaning it's time to turn leadership on its heel.

You have an advantage you didn't have before. Turns out the shoe fits. So why not wear it?

2 STEP OUT WITH FEMININE SWAGGER

In the last chapter you learned why women are uniquely positioned to shift the leadership paradigm. Today's young women can't imagine living under the rules and conditions my generation grew up with, or that our mothers survived. I stand back and admire the way my four nieces are living their lives. Waiting for that promotion? No way. They're going for it. Giving up their run or Pilates class to linger over their in-box? No more. They have boundaries. Breaking a glass ceiling? No need. The sky is their limit.

The trailblazers I met and interviewed for this book paved the way for this new generation by learning to stand tall and claim the lead. They've stepped into who they are, and move forward, willing to maneuver through—and occasionally jump right over—the barriers that cross their path.

They put their best foot forward. I call this "leading self," and it's an essential part of becoming the leader you were born to be.

Yet some women don't step forward into leadership.

Traditionally, this lack of progress has been attributed to the "glass ceiling"—that famous yet invisible barrier to advancement based on attitudinal or gender bias.

According to Catalyst, a non-profit organization, as of June 2014, there were 24 women leading Fortune 500 companies, including IBM and PepsiCo. That's up from seven in 2002–2003. Among the Fortune 1000 companies, there are twice as many, including the CEOs of Neiman Marcus Group, Cracker Barrel, and Dunn & Bradstreet.

Nonetheless, businesswomen still face hurdles. While 24 are Fortune 500 CEOs—a record high—that's only 4.8 percent of the total. And the figures hold for Fortune 1000 companies; fewer than 5 percent have a female at the helm. New to the list are Mary Barra of General Motors, Lynn Good of Duke Energy, Jacqueline Himan of CH2M Hill, Kimbery Bowers of CST Brands, Susan Cameron of Reynolds American Inc., and Barbara Bentler of Ross.

Having worked in technology for nearly 15 years, every time another woman scales the field's highest peaks, you can hear my heels jumping up and down in excitement!

It took a century for IBM, the male-dominated, blue suit–red tie giant, to appoint their first ever CEO who wears pumps, Virginia Rometty. Meg Whitman took the reins at Hewlett Packard, and the aforementioned Ursula Burns completed the technology triangle at Xerox. They joined the ranks of Safra Catz at Oracle, Marissa Mayer of Yahoo, and others. Marissa Mayer fell off the list when Yahoo failed to make the 2014 Fortune 500 listings for the first time in nine years. (I'm confident she will be back in the 2015 lineup.)

We are also represented in the ranks in energy (Duke, Graybar Electric, and Sempra Energy), food and agriculture (Archer Daniels Midland, Pepsico, and Campbell Soup), aerospace and defense (Lockheed Martin and General Dynamics), and others.

Information technology, consumer staples, and consumer discretionary industries have the highest percentage of women CEOs, tallying around 3 percent for each.

But there is a problem. Why aren't more women stepping forward in leadership?

Catalyst's women respondents reported the following top five barriers to advancement:

- Lack of significant general management or line experience (47%)

- Exclusion from informal networks (41%)

- Stereotyping and preconceptions of women's roles and abilities (33%)

- Failure of senior leadership to assume accountability for women's advancement (29%)

- Commitment to personal/family responsibilities (26%)

Participants in Catalyst's study also cited five success strategies that help women to overcome these barriers:

- Exceeding performance expectations (69%)

- Successfully managing others (49%)

- Developing a style with which male managers are comfortable (47%)

- Having recognized expertise in a specific content area (46%)

- Taking on difficult or highly visible assignments (40%)

Patricia Sellers, author and human rights activist, has spent a great deal of time writing about some of the world's most powerful women. She cites one specific quality that women have—a perceived need to be perfect—as the thing that prevents them from taking those risks that will elevate them on the path of influence. Being too afraid will lead to missed opportunities. Sellers asserts that power and influence will never come to the woman in executive leadership today unless she's prepared to move out of her comfort zone and just get over this fear.

The Lives and Times of the CEO, written by Ken Favaro, Per-Olka Karlsson, and Gary L. Meilson, predicts that in 2040 30 percent of today's college and business graduates will migrate to the role of CEO. Sixty percent of U.S. college students and 40 percent of MBA students are currently women.

So how can we prepare the future woman CEO? It is up to us women to prepare women for leadership while we are leading ourselves. If we release our own sense of imperfection we will allow our daughters, sisters, nieces and co-workers to realize their own perfection. If we step out of the shadow of measuring ourselves against a model that does not work for us, we will appreciate our brilliance and light the path for others to follow.

PUT ON YOUR GARDENING SHOES AND DIG UP THE ROOTS

At our lake house, there's a brick walkway along the side of the house that leads to the dock. One day, while I was walking there, I noticed that several of the bricks were uneven. While others lay evenly in place, two had shifted, rising above the level ground and creating an uneven and unsafe pathway.

What caused the bricks to shift? I thought the moss around the bricks might have caused them to lift so I bent down and started to dig at the moss. My husband noticed what I was doing and came over to look. He bent down, lifted up several bricks, and dug down with his hand into the soft ground, only to find a thick knotted tree root below. He gathered the hedge clippers in our small gray shed, clipped out the root, and put the bricks neatly in place once again.

What holds you back is the root under the walkway. The fears, the doubt, and the lack of decision keep us in place, uprooting our balance and keeping us off of our path.

Sometimes it isn't enough to remove the surface dirt in order to lay the bricks straight again. You have to dig deep and uproot whatever has unearthed them.

When I work with leaders I look for what lies beneath—the perceptions, beliefs, and fears that cause turmoil. Your core beliefs—those roots buried deep inside you—can send you into a state of upheaval from time to time. They can even uproot your successes—just when they are within reach.

It feels safer to stay just as is; it is normal to want to keep things just the same. Change is risky and takes courage to pursue. So does leadership.

Beliefs, perceptions, and the stories we tell ourselves lose power when you remember to rewrite them with new experiences.

So dig down deep, get your hands dirty, and uproot anything that holds you back. Work with a coach or mentor to help you change your beliefs and build new ones about yourself, your outlook on life, and your future.

Change your beliefs, and you will change any limiting thoughts, feelings, and behaviors, all in one single sweep. Don't let them block the path to leadership.

CHOOSING YOUR PATH OF LEADERSHIP

You have a choice in how you interpret the numbers. You might feel that the barriers are too difficult to overcome or it might be too ugly at the top to make the climb worthwhile. Or you can choose to look at these numbers as huge opportunities for your future.

Me? I am here to wave you on, and to challenge you, your business and your organization to stretch beyond what you think is possible. I know that there is a massive opportunity for women of all levels to step into and advance in leadership.

The path is paved for you to join other women making strides for success, even by taking a small step forward. Just as it isn't always easy being a woman, it isn't always easy to slip your delicate feet into the arches of a pair of stilettos.

But we still wear those high heels—because they elevate us, elongate our legs, define the muscles, optimize our appearance, attract attention, and command presence. It isn't easy to balance in heels but they give us a certain vantage point in business. Use that advantage to elevate your leadership.

Sometimes you have to feel the fear and move forward anyway.

I consider myself an edge walker. My whole life has been about stepping forward into uncertainty and into the edge of possibility. When you are standing on the edge, outside of your comfort zone, you wake up to all that comes into view and step into the pulse of what's possible.

You have to go to the edge, beyond what you currently know, and see what lies on the other side. The edge is scary for most people but it is where you can enjoy the most expansive vision. It is the transformational space where your potential, creativity, and innovation lie.

Sometimes walking away is a step forward.

At age 14 I learned what it means to be a Renegade.

I was walking beside my mother, and cars were whizzing by as we each carried a small bag of our belongings. I could feel the promise of summer in the breeze of the late spring air. With every step closer to freedom, hope heaved the weight of the last five years from my heart.

My mother and I were on our way, heading for a bus to our new and better lives. We were starting over, with my mother leading the charge.

While my confidence and optimism swelled the further we got from home, my mother's doubt grew insurmountable until it finally strangled her courage. Just steps away from our escape, she slammed shut our window of opportunity, turned around, and declared, "We're going back."

"Back" meant to my stepfather's commanding and controlling rules, rules I didn't understand. "Back" meant a life of quiet seclusion.

Until the age of 9, I lived in a residential neighborhood filled with friends of all ages. There was a park at the end of our road where we played kickball, and I'd belt out songs on the swing with my face lifted skyward and legs pumping as high as the swing would go. We played Old Mother Witch until the street lights came on and put on impromptu plays for our neighbors. I went to bed at night feeling the warmth of community, friends, and my small family consisting of my mother, my older sister, and me. My world changed at the age of 9 when my mother remarried.

That bright, happy world diminished into a mouse hole of darkness when we moved in with my stepfather.

Suddenly, I wasn't allowed to ride my bicycle around the circle of our neighborhood; I could only ride on one side of the street. There were few children nearby, and I wasn't allowed to have friends over or go to other children's houses. The summers were long and filled with quiet reading.

I was silently told to be seen and unheard and verbally told not to make any ripples in the water by asking for anything more than what was available to me. My voice on the swing was quieted, and I was forced to live in what felt like a box from which I could not escape.

The Renegade Leader inside of me was born the day we almost left my stepfather's world. I realized that my mother didn't have the resources or the courage to make a change. I realized that getting the life I wanted was going to be up to no one else but me.

So I was faced with a choice.

I could stay in a family in which I wasn't a fit, where I couldn't be myself, where my big life was very small. Or I could make a change and live life in my own shoes.

A year or so later, I did just that. One day after school, I gathered what belongings I could and packed them into my friend's car. As I left, I dropped a shoe on the marigold-lined sidewalk and didn't stop to pick it up.

That was the shoe that didn't fit.

I moved in with my best friend's family, became an emancipated minor, and continued on. It was my only choice. I was scared. I didn't know what was going to happen; I just knew I wanted the life I deserved.

As a result, I've made some out-of-the-box choices to get from where I was to where I wanted to be. I knew education was my way out of the life I didn't want, so I excelled at school and moved out the day after high school graduation, finding my own funding and resources to attend college and acquire two master's degrees.

This experience gave me a powerful lesson: It is easy to make a choice; it takes courage to act on it. To step forward and claim the life you know you deserve, to follow your heart instead of your head, even as it beats wildly.

PUTTING ON YOUR BIG-GIRL PUMPS

When you hear the word "renegade," you likely think of someone who doesn't play by the rules. This might pose a problem because, by and large, we women are taught at an early age to do just the opposite.

We are taught to play nice, to share, and to be helpful to others.

While we little girls were playing house together with our Easy Bake ovens and toy vacuums, the boys were outside playing sports—and playing to win. They were taught to be the quarterback and lead the team. We were taught to cooperate and support the team.

Of course, I've always been one of those people who questioned the rules. "Why?" was my constant query. Even at a young age, I remember my parents telling me that I only had so many words in my lifetime to say and if I kept talking I would run out much sooner than everyone else. So much of our conditioning comes from the past.

Myths or "rules" about women still exist. It's a mindset we can shift. I'm still questioning these beliefs. Read the "mindsets" below and implement the suggested actions that resonate with you.

Mindset #1: Women are invisible until they make themselves visible.

Being noticed is about being heard—something we, as women, are generally not taught to do. We're supposed to be good and wait to be rewarded. But getting noticed is about stepping up, speaking out, and being authentic. It isn't just about doing a great job managing the people who are beneath you and making sure work gets done; it's about reaching upward, finding a mentor, asking for new challenges, creating a network of people who believe in you, making sure everyone knows exactly what you've achieved, and—most importantly—*letting people know what you want.*

Strides for Success:

1. Brag. Do people know what you do? Report "what you do" by talking about "what is getting done." State, for example: "The report was completed on Wednesday and distributed, as promised." "I

organized the team's schedule so we could meet the project time line." "I stayed to complete the project late last night so the project would be done on time." "The client said they liked how I presented our product; I think they are going to buy." I recently attend a recognition award ceremony for top women in business. Five of the seven recipients diminished the value of the award, stating, "Thank you, but unlike the other women here, I was simply doing my job.... I don't deserve this. It really was my team that deserves the award.... What an opportunity. I am so grateful. Thank you, thank you." The other two proudly took the award and promoted the value of their organization, and one even added how she and her company were expecting to exceed expectations for next year, too.

2. Be a career strategist. Prepare for your performance reviews long before they are due. Track and report on your progress on the preset objectives for success. Plan your next step and ask your upper management or human resources for support on how to get there.

3. Put yourself on the stage even if you don't want the leading role. At least try out for it. You won't know what you want in your career until you investigate the possibilities. Wonder what becoming the regional director or the senior vice president would be like? Look into the job, interview for it, learn what you would need if you are not ready, knowing that you get to decide, if the job is offered, to say yes or no. Or you can do what my niece did: When offered an interim leadership position, she instantly moved her computer, her books, and her family pictures (her husband and two pugs) into the previous manager's office, staking claim before her official interview.

    Claim your next promotion as if it was the last item in your size on the Neiman Marcus annual sale rack. Run for it, grab it, and make it your own.

I've worked for six years in an organization providing executive coaching, leadership, and culture-building services with the CEO and the executive and the management team.

I was hired to help them to identify and groom their potential leaders for succession planning to executive roles. Two of my clients were from the same organization—a man and a woman, both with the same title, advancement opportunities, and similar longevity with the company.

The man said to me, "Let's use the coaching to figure out how I can advance. I want to make sure that I am seen as the right person for the next position. Let's work out a time line to make this happen."

The woman said, "I know I am capable of the position. I trust the company; they will promote me when they feel I'm successful. They will let me know when the time is right; they take good care of us."

I coached both to move forward. One asked me to; the other didn't. Who do you think got the job?

Mindset #2: Men take charge. Women take it personally.

I can't tell you how many times upper management has asked me to help a leader to "stop taking it personally." It is disheartening to see how much emotional energy is spent by leaders who rant and rave about those who have done them wrong, people they thought were friends but failed to be accountable, staff members who are determined to undermine and sabotage them, and how the looks and comments they receive from various people ruin their entire day. And it does, until they work with me. One thing you can't get back in life is your time; why waste it taking the actions of others personally?

Melanie is a new manager. When I first met her she told me she was disappointed with a new team member who was underperforming and purposely sabotaging her by making her look bad. His work "was awful," he seemed to be "incompetent," and he should have known better because he just "went through training." Her body was tense, and she looked angry and ready to cry at the same time.

A bit into our discussion I explained why she was exhausted: Emotion takes energy. First she had put on the heavy black judgment robe—"he was awful," judging his work as good or bad. Next she got out a label maker to label him as "incompetent." Lastly she got her report card, giving him an "F" for having failed his "training." Tiring, eh?

Strides for Success:

1. Words are just like particles in the air that you see through the sunlight of your window on a sunny day. Light and airy. They don't need to be weighed down by heavy emotion, judgment, or interpretation. Simply hear them as words, even if they appear to be pointed to you. Think of yourself as Teflon Woman and let them roll right off. "It is not about you" is a quote to remember. Every person's comment, observation, detail they provide is based on their perspective, their childhood experiences, and how they draw conclusions. When they are rough around the edges, it is because the experience they had with you triggered a memory from the past. You don't need to tolerate disrespectful behavior—but you don't need to add to its emotion, either.

2. Put a QTIP on your desk. I give them out to clients all the time: Quit Taking it Personally. Give them to your co-workers and your family members. Monitor your own self-thoughts. Are you layering in your perception to the situation? There are three truths: yours, theirs, and something in between. Just like the way dogs are unable to see the vivid colors in your couch upholstery, the

people around you have their own screens that limit their vision to how they see things. But the fact that people don't agree with you doesn't mean they are personally attacking you. If they say something to you that is painful, look below the words with empathy for their pain, and ask what triggered their behavior. Feel sorry for those whose ability to control is only through anger. How can you coach them to communicate differently? What can you model for them?

Mindset #3: Women are too soft, shying away from conflict.

My sister returned home from a long day at work. As she casually placed her pocketbook on the counter she noticed a message flashing on her telephone. The recording revealed an urgent request from her children's high school. They needed four dozen cookies baked and delivered by tomorrow afternoon for the teacher's appreciation event. My sister, spurred by the urgency immediately took out her mixing bowls. The problem is her youngest child had graduated two years before. Apparently she was never removed from the volunteer list.

If you are truthful with yourself you probably remember a time when you avoided conflict or let others overstep your boundaries. Practice using the word "no" or "no thank you" or "that's not a fit for me right now" until you get comfortable. Use the word "no" in your work conversations. You don't hesitate to say "No!" when your little darling tried to put a slice of pizza into the brand new Blu Ray player, or when a friend calls to go have drinks just as you are heading out the door for a great date. So why hesitate to say no something that does not align with your goals, beliefs or values?

Say no to doing the work that belongs to others, say no to people who don't respect your boundaries, and say yes to being in charge of your time and your career. Make your voice heard, stand your ground, think of conflict as any other conversation. You choose to say yes or you choose to say no.

Strides for Success:

1. Build your conflict muscle just as you would work on your abs at the gym; it takes repeated effort to make it easy to use.

2. Find the circle of consensus, the item(s) you do agree on. Begin your conflict conversation by stating what you both do agree on. Present the conflict and share your perspective—why you might have a different option. Ask the other person to look at his/her perspective through the lens of the shared circle of consensus and see what happens.

3. As I said before, words are just information, just like dust in the air—light and airy. Simply hear what is being said. Validate what you heard and then share your opinion. Avoid the words "you" and "I"; instead use "we both agree" once you have reviewed the shared circle of consensus. For example: "We both agree that hiring a candidate with a financial expertise will benefit our division. Mary has great leadership skills but does not have this experience. I can understand why you want her as a manager. Is this something we should compromise on if finances are such a key part of our success plan?"

Mindset #4: Women are great workers, but not great leaders.

Margaret Thatcher is one of the most famous female leaders in history. Yet this pioneering member of the female gender is also famous for saying, "If you want something said, ask a man. If you want something done, ask a woman."

I don't think she meant it as an insult. However, that same kind of thinking keeps women stuck in the "worker bee" roles that define middle management. Men, on the other hand, move seamlessly into the "speaking" roles associated with leadership. Because we care about people, it is easy to be lured into the minutia of the day-to-day at work instead of focusing on the more expansive role of leadership. Shift your view from the task orientation of leadership (the hands) to the heart (impacting people) and the head (establishing the vision for others to follow) to maximize leadership.

Strides for Success:

Break Your Own Rules: How to Change the Patterns of Thinking that Block Women's Paths to Power (Jill Flynn, Kathryn Heath, Mary Davis Holts; Flynn Heath Holt Leadership, 2011) determined six key mindsets women need to change in order to move forward in their leadership roles. These are those mindsets, along with the actions you can change to be seen for the leader that you are:

1. Focusing on others rather than making oneself a top priority. Make your career your priority.

2. Seeking approval rather than moving forward. I believe in "proceeding until apprehended." Bold women get noticed, so claim your space at whatever table you chose and keep the seat warm and active.

3. Being modest rather than "projecting personal power." Stand in your power, follow your intuitive guidance, know what you know, and claim it.

4. Working harder instead of "being politically savvy." Network with others. Establish a reputation for being an interesting person to be around.

5. Playing it safe rather than "playing to win." The results you create are your own. What you focus on expands, so why not focus on your success?

6. Believing it's all or nothing rather than "both-and." Compromise when you need to but ask for what you need; find the middle ground.

You know what is right for you, follow you own inner guidance system and trust that it will lead you where you want to be. Unlearn what you were taught and go with what you know. Catering to the messages of the past will not take you into the future.

EMBRACE YOUR BUNIONS

Bunions run in my family. A bunion, in case you're lucky enough not to have had one, is the bony part of your foot that can take on a life of its own by sticking out on the side of your big toe. My mother had them so badly she could hardly fit into a pair of shoes. My niece has them, yet walks the halls daily for her job in hospital administration.

And I have one that sticks out prominently on my left foot.

My sister laughs when we go shoe shopping and I tell her I have to have either a wide shoe to accommodate my bunion or an opening that allows it to peek out and see the world.

We all have our imperfections. As women and as leaders, we simply need to embrace our bunions as our own. Like my wide shoes or "bunion windows," you have to figure out your own work-around for your "lesser strengths." But as for your bunions themselves—those imperfections that drive you a little crazy—my advice is to embrace them.

Love yourself; feel comfortable in your own skin. No one else has what you have. Embrace who you are.

Lisa Nichols told me she hesitated to be a speaker for a long time. She failed English in school, was told she couldn't write or speak well, and also worried that, as an African-American woman, she wouldn't fit in with her "big hips and large lips."

Well, thank goodness she got over that. Not only did she build a multimillion-dollar business, she has reached millions of people, both nationally and internationally, with her powerful message of empowerment, service, excellence, and gratitude.

Her participation in the self-development phenomenon *The Secret* catapulted her popularity across the globe. Lisa has appeared on the *Oprah Winfrey Show*, *Extra*, *Larry King Live*, and NBC's Emmy Award–winning show *Starting Over*.

In addition, Lisa is the founder of Motivating the Masses and CEO of Motivating the Teen Spirit, LLC. Her transformational workshops have impacted the lives of more than 210,000 teens and more than 1 million adults. She has been honored with many awards recognizing her empowering work, including the Humanitarian Award from South Africa, the Ambassador of Good Will Award, the Emotional Literacy Award, and the Legoland Foundation's Heart of Learning Award. The mayor of Henderson, Nevada, has proclaimed November 20 as Motivating the Teen Spirit Day. And recently, the mayor of Houston, Texas, proclaimed May 9 as Lisa Nichols Day for her dedication to service, philanthropy, and healing.

None of this would have happened had Lisa stayed off the stage because of her "bunions." So leave yours behind and move forward, imperfections and all.

"To wear the shoes, and I mean really ROCK them, is to be
the foundation and be comfortable being that foundation, of

*yourself, of your position, or of your own company…and, of
course, your own life. Your shoes take you where you're going…
moving with you either forward or backward. They allow you
to stand tall or relax and walk slowly. To be the leader is to be
the seeker, the mover, and the motivator to others, and always to
yourself. Be the ear people will whisper in, be the number people
want to call, and be your own best and worst critic. Shoes say
a lot about a person that their mouths may never tell you, but
their inner being wants you to know."*

~ Nicole B.

Only you can determine where your shoes will take you.

Only you can give yourself permission to move forward, to be
seen for who you are, to let your brilliance out, to make your mark
on the world. Other people are too busy worrying about their own
performance to notice yours; you have to be the one to see yourself first,
and move yourself forward to the front of the line so you are noticed in
your organization as a leader in your industry, as a woman determined
to leave a heel print behind.

STEP OUT WITH FEMININE SWAGGER—
OR, THE SOFIA VERGARA EFFECT

Women have different reactions to the name Sofia Vergara.

Some roll their eyes. Some laugh with her during her award winning
best comedy series sitcom "Modern Family" every Wednesday night,
but then spend their 30-minute lunch break the following Thursday
discussing her with their colleagues.

Regardless of what they think, I'd be willing to bet the word
"entrepreneur" is probably the last word that comes to mind when they
think of her.

But that's precisely what she is, with a net worth reportedly around the $27 million dollar mark, very little of which comes from her work as an actress.

That makes Sofia Vergara a woman worth listening to when it comes to taking a few cues in how to drive your own success. So, how did she do it?

Her swagger.

And no, it's not the swagger you're thinking of!

It was 2013 when Sofia Vergara landed a coveted spot, with 99 other women, on *Forbes*'s list of the World's Most Powerful Women. And while many might think that her seemingly instant fame through the hit show *Modern Family* has everything to do with that, it doesn't. Plus, unlike the bureaucrats, the billionaires, and the philanthropists that she shares a spot on this list with, she is one of only 17 members of the group who are self-made.

Self-made?? Sofia Vergara? The actress?

No. Sofia Vergara. The entrepreneur.

At 40 years young, her list of corporate accomplishments includes endorsement deals with Diet Pepsi, Cover Girl, Kmart, and Rooms to Go.

But a lot of celebrities have endorsement deals. What makes Sofia Vergara's deals unique is the reasons behind them.

For example, she told *Lucky* magazine that she started working with Rooms to Go because her relationship with them started 15 years ago when she was a single mom and was able to furnish her home with affordable pieces from their stores.

She became the face of the thyroid medicine Synthroid not because it was a good business deal, but because she is a thyroid cancer survivor and wanted to be a part of the awareness campaign.

She also recently added a shapewear line to her list of corporate endeavors, and given the attention her own shape has received by the world at large, her net worth will probably take a nice boost from that venture as well.

In addition to all of this, she is the co-founder and CEO of a 17-year-old talent management company called LatinWE. And, oh yes, she also manages to find time to appear on TV once a week on an Emmy Award–winning sitcom.

How does she manage it all?

She's got swagger. A swagger that has not been dampened or softened by the fact that she is one of the few Latin-American women to ever make a *Forbes* list. In fact, her swagger has been fueled by the fact that she is a minority, in more ways than one.

The message is strong but we are too busy wiping noses and pulling dinner out of the oven in between client calls and e-mails to realize that those very qualities—the nurturing, caring qualities that make us women—will also make us successful leaders in business.

Sofia Vergara uses those assets to her fullest advantage, and she makes no apology for it. So why aren't the rest of us following suit?

Gayle Lemmon, contributing editor for *Newsweek*, started exploring the phenomenon of women, femininity, and leadership. She interviewed women in war-torn countries who have been making headway in their corporate cultures.

At a TED Talk, she compared those women to women in America—and made it very clear that, as a whole, we are doing it wrong.

Here (in America), words used to describe successful men in business include pioneer, innovator, and icon.

Women, on the other hand, do not receive the same accolades. Instead, we are more easily dismissed, and even sometimes ignored.

Lemmon postulates that swagger has everything to do with it. The only thing men are better at when it comes to leadership is just that: swagger.

Not that we can knock the men *completely* for that. Some of it really is simple biology, and it all boils down to that biochemical reaction that fuels swagger. It starts with testosterone, and the end product is aggression. Aggression has the Latin root *ag,* which means "before," and *gred,* which means "to walk" or "to step." So, men are simply better at stepping out, or swaggering out, in front of their female counterparts, because they have more testosterone in their blood than the woman they are competing with!

And we've taught men to swagger since their very first days. "Don't let anybody see you cry!" "Stop being such a Mama's boy!" "Step out and stand up for yourself!"

As a result, we've reared the men who are already swimming very easily in the stream up to the C-suite by helping them overvalue their strengths, all the while wondering how we can get there ourselves.

And, because the universe likes balance, the subconscious end result is we underrate our own qualities and stay precisely in the same position in the same stream that isn't moving at all.

Why?

We feel bad if we swagger because we lose sleep over the notion that it might send the wrong message.

Do you think those worries are keeping Sofia Vergara up at night?

Of course not.

Of course, you might be thinking none of this applies to you if you don't possess the "assets" that Sofia Vergara might have when she strolls into a contract meeting with Pepsi.

But it's time to stop thinking you don't have the assets. You do.

Researchers for a recent study in the *Harvard Business Review* have boiled it all down to one little word. And no, it's not "curves" or "sex appeal" (which is actually two words).

It's empathy.

In the last chapter, we looked at the study by researchers Jack Zenger and Joseph Folkman. They reported that in business, the personality profiles are very predictable. Historically men have been known to play to win, while women play to connect. If all you need to do to prevail is to prove that you are badder and bigger than the rest, then of course you will succeed at a faster rate.

Their findings concur with Gayle Lemmon's opinion that men overrate themselves while women underrate themselves. And that often boils down to the not-so-simple quality of aggression.

But, these researchers conclude, it *only* works if aggression—if being the biggest and the baddest—is all you need.

And they state, rather adamantly, that it isn't.

More and more researchers are telling us over and over and over again that we actually have *more* leadership skills than men. So why are women so underrepresented? Because we don't believe it. We don't believe that the things that make us so amazing as human beings are good enough to make us amazing leaders in business.

In fact, it is those very qualities that will land us in the C-suite.

For women, empathy *is* our swagger. Why are we hiding from it when all of the data clearly suggest it is working, and working very well, for those who know how to use it best?

How did Sofia Vergara get a national campaign for thyroid medicine? Empathy. How did she land a contract that enabled her to change the way women view their own curves and shape? Empathy. How did she launch a multimillion-dollar endorsement deal with a furniture company she used to shop from when she was a single mom? Empathy.

Being humble, creative, honest, compassionate, caring, and kind is not a bad thing in business. When you use them right, those qualities are going to turn heads. For Sofia Vergara, that is precisely the case, approximately 27 million times and counting.

So what do you do to succeed? As Nancy Mills will soon share, know you are "enough" and begin from there. Trust that, as a woman, you have what it takes. You can leave behind every compromise, see possibilities in challenges, and create amazing work experiences by taking charge of your career, business, and life. The first step in leading self is to know your assets, what you need to acquire, discard, or step away from and how to emerge powerfully.

Rules may have power to hold women back, but the great thing about rules is they were made to be broken. Especially if you're a Renegade.

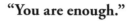

"You are enough."

Meet Nancy Mills, CEO Spirited Women

"Spontaneity sometimes really is the name of the game. So I was out walking in Playa Vista, CA, a place I call home several months of the year, when Debora called. I decided to keep walking until I entered Playa Vista's Ballona Wetlands Discovery Park, a park dedicated to the history of the Tongva Indians who originally lived on the land—and one of the few tribes that had a woman leader!

"There I was in this magical setting, sitting underneath the wooden teepee and listening to the birds talk and fly, all the while feeling the ancestral energy so influenced by the strength of women tribal leaders. What a fitting time to talk about women running in high heels and moving forward. I was in heaven! I felt the words flow through me. And I realized sometimes the best interviews are the ones where the Creator takes over. And of course, spontaneity."

"You are enough...just as you are," Nancy exclaimed without hesitation at the start of our interview. She wants all women, girls, and older women to breathe that in and to know it as their truth. Nancy, the passionate CEO of Spirited Women, advocates for women to stand out instead of blending in. *"Travel to the beat of your own drum; we all have an inner light that will guide your passion."*

"Women are often guided in a direction, to find the 'right job' or work for the 'right company' or the 'right partner.' Sometimes they can lose themselves along the way." There is so much more to life. *"Women don't set out to be influencers; they don't wake up and say I am going to impact the world. Even J.K. Rowling, creator of the Harry Potter books, didn't set out to write a book that would capture the interest of millions; she wrote quietly for herself and her enjoyment."* Nancy's advice: *"To begin with, women need to keep moving forward and to know regardless the goal you choose, know you are good enough and you can do it."*

No matter where you are in leadership know you are good enough. Leading from a powerful leadership presence means being confident in your strengths and being willing to add the competencies you need, when you need them.

Just as your heels become more comfortable with wear, so does leadership. When you push yourself beyond your comfort zone you, like your shoes, begin to stretch. With enhanced leadership skills you can walk easier and farther, making the journey from the break room to the boardroom with equal ease.

In a world of distrust in leadership, employees feel safer with leaders who take initiative, challenging what doesn't feel right, and are willing to try out new innovative ideas. Leaders who practice self-development and show vulnerability make it easier for employees to be honest and to ask for what they need. Leaders who walk their talk model the way for others to follow. In coaching I call this "leaders go first."

Now I invite you to Lead Forward by walking you through the steps of the L.E.A.D. Forward Formula™.

3 THE L.E.A.D. FORWARD FORMULA™: FOUR STEPS TO SUCCESS

You've read about the state of leadership today and learned why you are best positioned to lead the way. Now learn how you can step into the heels of a Renegade Leader, and lead forward.

Meet Robin Comstock,
President and Past CEO, Chamber of Commerce

"I learned in 8th-grade drama class that there is no performance without an audience."

"You have to align people to the vision to be able to succeed." Robin learned along the way that leadership is like theatre; you have to create the persona of the position, even if you are just learning your lines. *"In order to be trusted by others as a leader, you need to create the persona of authority, graciousness, leadership, and vision."*

For more than 25 years, Robin has served as executive director of a vast city's chamber of commerce. She realizes that all eyes are on her and, at any moment, media and stakeholders expect results—results she could not produce without her stellar team to support and invest in her as their leader. *"I wouldn't be held high unless there were hands to hold me,"* she laughs.

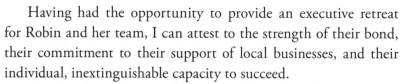

Having had the opportunity to provide an executive retreat for Robin and her team, I can attest to the strength of their bond, their commitment to their support of local businesses, and their individual, inextinguishable capacity to succeed.

So many leaders tell me they are tired of the "drama." Robin understands that a leader has to manage the theatrics, the production, and the characters as well as give direction. *"Much of the work is done behind the scenes, in the office, with close team members so that when you enter the podium at your annual meeting, the conference room with your stakeholders, you envision yourself in the role of capability.*

"Enter the stage with confidence for others to believe you are a leader. Enter the 'theater of the moment' and wear the persona (even if it doesn't fit yet) of the behaviors and the attitudes that drive people to believe you are the leader."

As we sat eating our lunch at a favorite restaurant, I asked Robin to tell me more about how to plan for success. *"Women need to understand the difference between what happens behind the scenes and what happens on stage. Use your behind-the-scenes crew to support you so you show up on stage as a top performer."*

Leadership isn't easy. *"Let the discomfort of failure become comfortable. A leader needs to not only handle the social, emotional, and intellectual processes of other people but also in themselves."*

Robin has an unwavering belief in making the impossible possible, and with the vast number of events and services her organization provides, she somehow seems to accomplish just that. She learned along the way, *"If you are not at the table, your voice will not be heard."*

Robin's advice: *"For women to achieve what they want, they need to find the cracks, windows, and doors to walk through, to make their way in and make their presence be known. Like a great actor, people believe what you project, and your behaviors effect how people perceive you."*

In preparation for writing *Running in High Heels,* I not only researched all of the recent leadership studies and interviewed women across the country, I sat back and thought of each coaching engagement experienced over the past 12 years, I began to weave together the common threads that created results with each leader, each team, each organization. My entire dining room was filled with flip charts and sticky notes of every color. I tracked every action and every result and soon I began to see the pattern. This became the L.E.A.D. Forward Formula™, an acronym for each step of leadership progressing from self-leadership, to leading others, to leading an organization, and lastly to standing out and distinguishing yourself or your business as the leader of the pack. As I looked at the formula in detail I remembered every pain point my clients expressed, the dreams they hoped to realize, and the pervasive thoughts that kept them up at night.

Maybe you picked up this book because you want to be a better leader.

Or, in an effort to be a leader you are frustrated by the continual challenges you are seeing across departments, racing to put out fires, feeling overwhelmed by demands, and noting the few items on your to-do list checked off at day's end. Every department, every person seems to need your attention.

Does it feel a little bit like a game of whack-a-mole?

Perhaps you are a leader in name but you know deep down inside the impact you can make can be so much bigger.

You have come down this path in leadership.

You have a vision you want to achieve, but things are not happening fast enough—or you are feeling stale, are frustrated with the people part of leadership, or hate leading, but you know this is a door you have to go though in order to achieve your results and for your vision to materialize.

It's time to stretch.

To take a leap.

It could be a project you've been given.

Or a newly inherited executive role.

Or your own organizational initiative.

Today's business climate is like a freight train and you sense you need to do something different just to keep up but might not be sure what it is.

I'm here to help you to lead forward by exploring the competencies you need to confidently succeed no matter what position you hold. It begins with the L.E.A.D. Forward Formula™.

The L.E.A.D. Forward Formula™
Four Stiletto Strategies

It's been said that life is all about how you show up. As Robin said, how you present yourself to others sets the tone for how they will show up as well. We know leadership isn't easy. All leaders have a goal, a vision they are trying to achieve. They ask, "How do I get from where I am to where I want to be?"

I get my best ideas in the shower. If you are like many of my clients your time in the shower isn't spent dreaming about your next vacation, or your upcoming spa treatment. Instead you are thinking about work. Wondering how you are going to get your team on the same page. You are thinking about Mary and why she doesn't understand "good enough" is *never* good enough. You envision Marc's blank stare, which you've never been able to break, and you worry about the upcoming meeting, knowing you will be the only one talking in the conference room while everyone sips their coffee like a rich liqueur.

Given the statistics this is not going to change unless we lead diffently.

A recent Kellogg advertisement said it beautifully: "Seeing the future isn't so difficult when you are the one creating it."

Businesses need to become alive again. To get people excited about the work that they do. Too many leaders are bogged down with what they see, lack of accountability, high turnover, or an inability to attract and retain talent. But the problem is deeper than that.

There is a fault in business, a fracture that lies beneath what is visible. It's what lies beneath that shuts down the conversation in the conference room, that provokes resistance with every change, and it's this lack of luster that keeps ideas from growing from creation to innovation.

My clients know I fix what is visible as they get results; what they might not realize is that the majority of my work is done below the surface, pulling up the root cause like an unwanted vine, creating a nurturing soil for innovation, collaboration, and creativity to flourish.

The L.E.A.D. Forward Formula™ takes into consideration the need to evolve, to shift the paradigm of leadership, to be current, relevant, and 10 steps ahead of the game. It is designed to produce game-changing results, results my clients have witnessed again and again. And it is meant to be easy, providing paint-by-numbers suggestions based on experience instead of theory.

Best of all, it doesn't require a brigade of consultants filling your hallways and taking root in your offices.

I realize you have a job to do: to lead your team, department, business, or company, or to simply harness the power of you own career. Your time is valuable. It's my goal as a coach not to build interdependence, but to give you, your team, and your organization access to tools that will assist you on the road to success.

The L.E.A.D. Forward Formula™ includes four steps, each offering its own framework. In the next four chapters you will read about each one. When we work with leaders, with their teams, and within organizations we identify which steps are relevant to produce sustainable results, customizing each solution to your unique needs.

Many leaders would love to lead forward with influence, impact, and ingenuity. The biggest problem innovative leaders have is how to align others to their vision; how do you get everyone on the same page? Sometimes there are gaps in communication; we help you communicate powerfully in order to excite, ignite, and fuel the passion in your people. Leaders know they need to influence but many don't know how to flex influence to maximize results. We help leaders get an idea accepted across the organization or build their sphere of influence. By building a personal brand and a power base, leaders benefit by gaining distinction as a thought leader, and promotions come naturally, and they are able to motivate high performance within their teams and organization.

All leaders have the potential to become extraordinary leaders.

With the L.E.A.D. Forward Formula™ you will have courage to trust your gut, embrace change, and take action on innovative ideas. You will lead with influence and get your teams on board with your big vision. Your teams will perform and communicate better. Your message will be heard, understood, and acted upon, and collaboration replaces conflict. Your organization will gain the opportunity to increase profits, while creating a culture that people are excited to be a part of.

Leadership becomes easier. When you master the elements within the L.E.A.D. Forward Formula™ you will lead powerfully and authentically, managing up, down, and across the organization with confidence.

Now, I promise to take you to the learning edge of personal development and the leading edge of business where you will see a fuller vision for yourself, your teams, and your organization.

The L.E.A.D. Forward Formula™ begins with "L" for Leverage. Leadership is a muscle you have to work. You know the value of doing squats, leg lifts in the shower, or a few power abs during a commercial. In an ever-evolving business world, why would you think a degree, a resume of experience, or a title would keep you in leadership shape?

Leverage means to put leadership into action. Leadership likes to be seen.

Leadership wasn't meant to be kept in a frame, hidden in your cubicle, or experienced only in the boardroom.

Leadership is your swagger—your way of walking, breathing, thinking, and behaving when you come in and when you go out the threshold of your business.

"**L**" is for leveraged leadership. You work it. You will learn how to communicate powerfully, engage in a deeper level of influence, and build a power base to support you.

"**E**" is for Engage. Success doesn't happen alone. You need your people on board. You need a culture that rallies around shared goals and demonstrates its values in day-to-day behaviors. You need a team that is just as excited about your vision as you are, standing ready to make a positive impact on the bottom line. It is up to you to move people to passion, positivity, and possibility. Learn how to engage and mobilize your teams, get everyone on the same page, and increase performance, productivity, and positivity.

"**A**" is for Activate. Many leaders complain about their culture not realizing their responsibility in creating it. Activate will share the secrets of activating a high-performance culture built upon the foundation of trust, courage, and innovation. Top leaders take responsibility for driving the company culture with collaboration, joint leadership, transparent communication, and innovation. Here you will learn the key attributes of how to have a culture that people are happy to be a part of.

Lastly is "**D**" for Distinguish. It's not enough to blend in; its more fun to to stand out, as a leader, and as an organization. Every leader has a brand; it's up to you to distinguish yours and that of your organization. Distinction is alluring. People want to get to know you. Your teams are excited to accelerate past your competition. Here you will learn about how your story, your brand, and your message result in becoming the leader others choose to follow.

The L.E.A.D. Forward Formula™ was developed to empower you to think, behave, and lead differently. To break away from the norm—what is expected—and to step into what could be amazing.

As a Renegade myself I'm always looking for "nowhere near the box" problem-solving ideas.

I tracked down the key steps that were game changing. These became the L.E.A.D. Forward Formula™ for Leaders and the I.N.F.L.U.E.N.C.E. Framework™ previously published in *The Renegade Leader* (excerpts of which are found in the "Activate" chapter).

When I proposed these solutions, leaders I work with didn't believe what I said to be true. They crossed their arms and stood their ground, stating firmly, "Change can't happen, not with the people and culture I have." They shook their heads, eyes dreary from lack of sleep, and confessed, "I have no time for this; I can hardly get to what I need to do, let alone take on any more." Others blamed the economy for the just getting by and some succumbed to wanting to find the exit door themselves.

A few looked at me with disbelief. Is it possible?

I know it's not only a possibility, but attainable.

Imagine a company in which the positive energy is palpable. Evolving and money-making go hand-in-hand. Your team collaborating together and creating new pathways for success. Picture an environment where success is contagious, and everyone is committed to the shared vision—your vision.

Imagine having the time to enjoy your success and feeling richly satisfied at day's end.

Now, imagine this is true of your business—*every day.*

Clients who have worked with me have won awards, while increasing their profits many-fold and receiving recognition for their leadership roles—all while enjoying their own authentic version of success.

But best of all?

They are leading their companies in ways they had previously only dreamed of. My clients:

- Take four-week vacations at Martha's Vineyard and the company runs without them.

- Have the time to travel to Europe with their kids to experience the culture.

- Dance on the beaches of New Mexico while their executive team penetrates new markets.

- Create their personal brand without the company brand.

- Become bestselling authors and sought-after speakers at industry events.

- Refresh, rejuvenate, and revamp in Bali to spur their creativity.

- Celebrate their success by giving back within the community.

- Experience a gravity-defying level of confidence in themselves, their organizations, and their potential.

Profits, performance, positivity, and freedom from the confines of leadership can be your reality, too.

Just follow my lead, with the L.E.A.D. Forward Formula™ and lead with influence, impact and ingenuity.

$\mathcal{L}$EVERAGE: HOW TO LEAD WITH A POWERFUL AUTHENTIC PRESENCE

The L.E.A.D. Forward Formula™ begins with "L" for "Leverage: How to Lead with a Powerful Authentic Presence.

The Renegade in Heels story below illustrates how the three steps below can reshape a career trajectory and help you to be seen, heard, and noticed on the leadership runway.

1. *Be seen. Keep yourself visible...develop your power base.*

2. *Be heard. Say what you want to say...communicate powerfully.*

3. *Get noticed. Own the stage...claim your spotlight.*

Nicole: A Renegade in Heels

As a young professional Nicole stands at 5' 1", but because she wears very high heels she is seen and her presence is known everywhere she goes. Matter of fact, each time she arrives in my office lobby the staff at the front desk looks over the reception desk to check out her shoes. If it isn't the clatter of her shoes that draws attention, it is the radiance of her personality.

I first came to know Nicole as a participant in the leadership training I was providing to her organization; she was one of 60 managers in attendance. I noticed that she playfully added flavor to her teammate with her powerball of energy as she readily participated in the training and its role-play exercises.

"As the youngest member of our executive team," Nicole explains, *"I spent a lot of time watching, listening, and learning from people I was trying to be just like. I looked up to these people based on their credentials, age, time with our company, and many more reasons.*

"I always felt a little 'off,' however, because, as much as I admired these individuals, I realized I didn't want to be just like any one of them—or just like anyone as a matter of fact."

I next saw Nicole when I facilitated a team performance workshop for her and her team, providing coaching on how to overcome the obstacles noted in their team assessment and build from their strengths. In this smaller group, Nicole had a voice—a strong voice—and asserted her ideas on how the team could improve their performance.

The following year, the organization identified high-potential leaders I would work with for private coaching. I was so excited to see Nicole's name on my list. In the privacy of my office, Nicole expressed her true desire. As a corporate executive chef and newly assigned marketing director, she had a passion for her organization to be successful and had a burning desire to leave her own heel print not only in the legacy of her New England–based company, but in that of the nation. Nicole was determined to make her dream a reality.

Several times each month she sat in her office as members of the executive leadership team filed into the conference room. With serious looks on their faces and armed with notes and laptops, they looked ready to make forward strides. Here she knew decisions were being made, plans for the future formed, and problems solved. She longed to have a seat at that table.

Have you ever had that burning desire, that driving intuition in your stomach, but felt unsure if you should express it? That is exactly what Nicole was experiencing.

Getting a seat on the executive team became our first coaching objective. Nicole and I reviewed her ideas and identified where they met the shared interests and decision criteria of the executive team. Having worked with the CEO for some time, it was easy for me to align what would fit for the executive team. Now we simply needed to get their attention.

I assisted Nicole in building her playbook, a clear plan of action to position herself as the missing piece of the leadership puzzle. A leader in name—corporate executive chef and marketing director—yet not yet recognized to be at the big table.

We worked hard, putting out heads together and writing out pages of notes until we had her approach just right. I crafted her sound bites—why she belonged at the table and the impact she could have if given a seat.

As with any change, resistance always raises its head. Our minds and bodies like to keep up the status quo, screaming against any change. Nicole had some reservations. Oh no, FEAR (False Events Appearing Real) claimed a space on our agenda.

So we simply gave her inner critic (yes, ladies, we all have one!) a seat in my office and gave it permission to have a voice. We heard its concerns, answered what we could, and sent it on its merry way.

Nicole requested time with the executive team. Our plan worked and her meeting was scheduled. I held my breath in my office that day, mentally aligning myself with her and sending good vibrations her way. I knew she was nervous, but she was prepared and supported by her many notes, her key bullet points, and her platforms shoes.

I jumped for joy in celebration; she got it—a seat at the executive table! Although not everyone might have been convinced, the CEO was impressed with her presentation, her courage, and her confidence. Her message was heard.

Nicole asked me to share her advice with you. *"After working with Debora, I realized that I was sitting at that table because I was me, and no one else. I had the advantage of being able to soak in all of my team members' years of experience, learn from their mistakes, see how they all individually approached things, and collect all of their genius. I transitioned under her guidance from someone who was at the table, to someone who showed up at the table, and I work on that continuously. No one will push you through the ranks; at some point, you need to develop into who you are, put your 'inner critic' in a strait jacket and lock it in the closet, and own your seat at the table."*

Yet, as Nicole indicated, sitting at the big table is not the same as owning your seat at the table and showing up and being heard—putting your big ideas out there without worry of rejection and claiming your space in the world.

Nicole got what she wanted by tracking the results she had produced in her marketing role; she brought in her new ideas, launched creative campaigns, and produced financial results. She had earned her seat at the table.

To sum up, *"After being coached by Debora, I understood that I was at that table because those people I so admired actually admired me, too. Once you empower yourself, the world is like a whole new place. My time with Debora and Renegade Leader Coaching has undoubtedly benefited my career, my relationships, and me as a person. I have gained invaluable life 'tools' that will help me dig my way to where ever it is I want to go."*

"I was raised to be independent," says Nicole, *"and I have an equal partnership at home. But when you're a young woman thrown into a male-dominated business, you start to question yourself. Debora made me believe.*

Now I know I haven't reached my goals by chance but because of who I am. Debora gave me the tools to be successful and still be me."

Nicole summarizes her journey this way: *"I went from being nervous about coaching—thinking, 'Is this a nice way to tell me I need some skills?'—to thanking our CEO so much for giving me these tools."*

Imagine speaking up, being seen in your radiant brilliance, being noticed for your contributions, and having your message be heard and be acted upon. Yes, doesn't that feel good?

So what did Nicole do to Leverage her leadership and show up powerfully as her authentic self?

She used three key strategies we deliver with clients who want to want to be seen, heard, and noticed: the skill set to communicate powerfully, influence others, and develop your power base.

Communicate Powerfully So Your Message Is Heard, Understood, and Acted Upon

Communicating powerfully is key for anyone in business. We don't do our work alone. Your message needs to be understood by your customer, your employees, your stakeholders, your teams, or those who share your cubicle space. It doesn't matter if you sit at the head of the boardroom table or on the side of your family table: Communication is key.

Leadership at its core is communication; it is an integral part of all of our engagements. Think of how much of your time is spent:

- In one-on-one communication.

- Leading meetings.

- Asking for accountability.

- Moving conversations forward to results.

- Getting ideas accepted across an organization.

- Public speaking.

- Crafting social media messages.

- Ensuring everyone is aware of the organization's media sound bites.

- Identifying how to choose the right communication style for the situation.

- Modeling the desired culture of the organization through its messages.

- Building strong working relationships up, down, across, and outside the organization.

- Translating between technical knowledge and business results.

- Building strong alliances and partnerships with others through communication.

And if you really want your voice heard, like many of my clients, it means communicating as thought leader, taking a stand on what political or business changes affect your industry, sitting on your industry board, and affecting change by having your voice be heard by your employees, consumers, industry, and the media. Developing your messages for effective communication requires much more than a $99 public speaking seminar. As we have seen in recent times, executives are dismissed easily with a few words misspoken.

That's not the biggest risk. The biggest risk is not having your message heard, understood, or, worse, acted upon. Lack of follow-through and accountability are the perennial complaints among leaders. Not knowing how to have a message that enrolls and motivates others to your vision is equally painful. The risk is high. Messages that are confusing build mistrust, starting a hairline crack in your trust foundation that will only widen with time. Requests for accountability that are not clear leave projects uncompleted, deadlines missed, costly projects, and dissatisfied customers in their wake. Not having a message that is equally heard across divisions causes silos, divisions within the company, and polarizes the workforce. If you are experiencing missed deadlines, resistance, lack of accountability, and drama in the workplace, refocus on communication.

What surprises me the most is that most of the time leaders don't know why this is happening. Few associate it with communication.

Language is the bridge from where you are to where you want to be.

Unfortunately for most women, it is also the place where we can trip up the most. But it isn't our fault. We speak differently. When we had "the talk" in health class no one told us that in addition to physical differences, men and women communicate differently. My clients tell me that language is my "golden ore." I am forever coaching them on how to deliver effective messages, communicate clearly in e-mails, and navigate through difficult conversations so that they can achieve their goals.

UNDERSTANDING THE GENDER GAP (COMMUNICATING WITH MEN, WOMEN, OR BOTH)

Much research supports the idea that men and women have different communication styles. Since communication is what links leaders to their followers, being aware of these differences is helpful to all leaders.

It isn't a matter of thinking like a man or a woman, but of talking like a leader. Words have the power to undermine leadership, or to confirm it.

The study of language also shows that in addition to the style of communication, men and women have a different purpose in communicating. Academic research on psychological gender differences indicates women use communication as a tool to enhance social connections and create relationships; men use language to exert dominance and to drive tangible outcomes.

This is why women tend to have more expressive, tentative, cooperative, and polite communication characteristics, while men use more aggressive, assertive, direct, and powerful communication.

Women also have more to say. It has been claimed that women speak about 20,000 words a day—some 13,000 more than the average man. Women like to explain *why* an action is needed; male leaders focus on *what* action needs to take place. We frame a picture with lots of description; men just share the snapshot. You want to provide the story; they just want the headline. This gap might be why men tune out. They really don't hear what you have to say, or you lose trust as all the details only seem to appear as excuses instead of background narrative. I often wonder if this why women receive less funding from venture capitalists: Do we talk too much at the meetings?

In *The Female Brain,* Dr. Louann Brizendine notes the neurobiological differences in men and women:

> *In the brain centers for language and hearing, for example, women have 11 percent more neurons than men. The principal hub of both emotion and memory formation—the hippocampus—is also larger in the female brain, as is the brain circuitry for language and observing emotions in others. The female brain has tremendous unique aptitudes—outstanding verbal agility, the ability to connect deeply in friendship, a nearly psychic capacity to read faces and tone of voice for emotions and states of mind, and the ability to defuse conflict. All of this is hardwired into the brains of women. These are the talents women are born with that many men, frankly, are not.*

This ability to "read" people more easily gives you a leadership advantage. Rebecca Rockafellar, general manager of iStockphoto, believes, *"Women have a natural tendency to both pay attention to work and also observe the reactions of those around them…. Women file away facial expressions and body language a bit more closely. Instead of discounting that social intuition, I think we should use what we see in our relationship to create a more bonded team."*

This is why women have the ability to not just lead but serve as great leaders. This skill gives you an intuitive edge—to gain access to more information about your employees, your teams, and your customers, and to use that information to guide your business decisions. I've been hired by male CEOs who said they wanted a "female perspective" to gain a better understanding about their people and how to position their company for the woman consumer. Women are naturally wired to be transformational leaders, building the collaboration and trust-engaged cultures needed to create sustainable businesses in a modern economy.

And we do it through communication. In this framework the key to effective communication means understanding the differences and how to navigate them, developing a clear message of communication, building the language of accountability, and providing inspirational messages to motivate and engage. I also like to help leaders develop the language of vulnerability—how to share when things are not going well, when they don't have the answers, when they need the people on the ground floor to share what they think the company should do next.

What happens when you sharpen your communication skills? You:

- Become more competent in influencing other people to improve results.

- Translate between technical language and business outcomes, so that people outside technical realms will want to listen.

- Lead teams based on informal influence, not formal title.

- Build strong working relationships up, down, across, and outside the organization.

- Improve overall leadership presence and impact, and have more credibility and trust within the organization.

Strides for Success:

Colleague Suzanne Bates notes eight communication skills CEOs need to have in *Speak Like a CEO: Secrets to Commanding Attention and Getting Results that Will Help Any Leader Speak Effectively and Win Over the Audience:*

1. Talk about big ideas. Every speech or presentation needs one big idea that gets people excited and interested, and makes you memorable.

2. Speak in the moment. No one likes a canned speech. Get your finger on the pulse of what your audience is thinking about.

3. Keep it simple. Many speakers try to do too much. Your message should be simple and straightforward to be remembered.

4. Be a straight shooter. To speak like a leader, your message must ring true. Your audiences have a "truth radar."

5. Be an optimist. When you're the leader, people look to you to tell them what is possible.

6. Focus on the future. In good times and bad, people look to you to lay out a plan.

7. Be real. If you're a leader with a big title, you have one strike against you. You need to be authentic to connect.

8. Stand for something. People aren't just going to work for a paycheck. Let them know your values—and why their work matters.

Many leaders know what they are supposed to be speaking about; however, many struggle with how to say it. Communication has been the backbone of my training, in sales, as a psychotherapist, and as a business and executive coach. Almost every class, workshop, or long-term training I've been involved in has been about how to use effective communication to engage, motivate, and establish a trusting rapport with my clients.

Leaders can't succeed without clear communication to their employees, stakeholders, and industry leaders. The American Management Association (AMAWorld, Summer 2011) identified 44 competencies as critical for effective management development, noting that the ability to master crucial conversations didn't only predict managerial effectiveness; it was one of the most potent drivers of organizational performance.

Influencing Others

Nicole had to communicate powerfully to be heard; knowing what to say allowed her the ability to influence others. Influence is another framework we build with our clients to gain influence in and outside of their organization.

Do you want to have more impact, enjoy the feeling of accomplishing your goals, and strengthen your relationships while you are doing it?

Leveraging your leadership gets you seen; communicating powerfully gets your message heard and acted upon; influencing allows to you to enroll others in your vision and to impact change.

The problem is influence can be thought of as manipulative, just as salespeople are frozen in place when it comes time to have a sales conversation. I've written about influence for decades. I see influence as co-creating solutions that result in a decision that is far better than the contribution of any one individual. What I most often see is that leaders don't plan on how they are going to influence others.

You influence every time you get dressed in the morning. You choose your clothes and your shoes; you get to decide how you want to be perceived based on your appearance. Why not think the same way about leadership?

The most successful leaders influence others to embrace and implement their ideas.

Unfortunately, even at the top levels of an organization, many leaders are under the false impression that there is only one way do this. Others avoid trying to influence as they believe it might lead to conflict. Without knowing how to influence:

- It is harder to get things done up, down, and across the organization.

- It feels like everyone isn't on the same page about expectations.

- Leading an organization is more frustrating and less fulfilling than it has to be.

You can only influence effectively if you know what style of influence engages your interest and how to flex to the key drivers of the person you are speaking with.

Influence goes beyond deep listening skills; instead you listen to understand which of seven influence styles are going to work. Use this knowledge to understand how to communicate and enroll another person to your point of view or your goal or to co-create a new commonality.

There is an art and a science to influence, to know the right conversations to have in order to get results, and keep the relationship strong.

Strides for Success:

Read each description below and identify which type of influence drives engagement for you personally. Are you a results-oriented person, do you need a visual picture, or do you make decisions based on your gut? Write down your style.

Next name a member of your team. Read the descriptions below and note the key driver for that individual. This is especially interesting if you selected someone you have conflicts with. What can you do, knowing his/her influence style, to enroll him/her in your ideas by matching his/her influence style? The good news is that our styles are not fixed; you can flex to the style of communication that you know will be most effective for your message to be heard.

Driven by execution, results, and business outcomes? The left brain is the seat of facts, logic, analysis, information, and data. When you know facts that matter to the other person, use these items to gain his/her interest.

Driven by vision, creativity, and innovation? The right brain is where we process images, stories, metaphors, and pictures. It is the gateway to the subconscious. By using more stories with a visual person you will engage his/her brain to enroll in your vision.

Driven by intuition? The gut, or "hara" as the Japanese call it, is our center. It is where we go when we take a stand, negotiate, assert appropriately, create a contract, or set boundaries. Ask an intuitive person how they "feel" about your idea and you will get their honest answer.

Driven by people, impact, and heart? In situations where we want authentic commitment and not just compliance, it is not enough to tell or assert. To enroll a heart centered person discuss the people impact of any idea.

Driven by collaboration and community? Here, we appeal to our common ground and the bonds that hold us together.

Driven by vision? Vision is about where we are going. Here, the leader paints a compelling, inspiring picture about where we can go together, and then invites others to jump in and build on the vision. This is the approach to use for a team that is kicking off or when a push is required to get people to move forward despite challenges. If you combine the right brain, spirit, and vision, you can make a compelling case that gets a team aligned in a powerful, authentic way.

Driven by avoidance? Yes, sometimes the legs are the most powerful tool—walking away. The legs are used when conversations start to go poorly. This doesn't mean that you give up and retreat, but does mean that you take some time to excuse yourself, let both parties rethink their positions, and come back together. The Harvard Negotiation Project calls this "Going to the Balcony." It prevents a meeting from spiraling downward.

Clients wonder how I am able to "profile" to craft the best way to communicate with another individual, team, or partner organization I've never met. I'd like to say it is magic or a special gift, but it's not. Simply said, I ask enough questions to understand the style of my client as well as to understand the probable profile of the party they are trying to influence. From here I script out the conversation that will produce results.

What style of influence will work best for the team member you have in mind? Next, plan your influence conversation. What is in it for them? What do you know you both agree on? Use that to begin the conversation.

Develop your Power Base

Nicole had to modify her presentation to influence each member of the team as well as the team as a whole. She also leveraged her relationships, using her coach as her power base and her trusted relationship with the CEO.

To effectively manage your career at any level you need to communicate powerfully, understand how to align for influence, and next develop a power base. As part of our coaching we assist clients in identifying and building a strong power base. A power base includes the people, organizations, or enterprises that would support you on a moment's notice. These are people you nourished relationships with; beyond mentoring, it is an active engagement of collaboration and support. Men tend to build their power bases on the golf course; some women, too. If you don't golf you are going to have to look for ways to build your power base, even seeking out and making initial contacts to do so.

An invaluable part of leveraging leadership is developing your power base. Some leaders do this naturally; others are new to taking the time on this activity. What I do know is that those who understand that developing supportive relationships is invaluable escalate their careers and are seen as powerful leaders. In the world of technology, don't be fooled into thinking you have a power base because of the number of Facebook fans or LinkedIn collaborators. We have moved to this very superficial approach to networking, making contacts, and building our power base. And it's almost like there's this illusion that, if we have lots of connections and we reach out to people that way, we have a strong power base. Unfortunately nothing could be further from the truth.

Your power base consists of people who can support you in your next promotion. They can connect you to the resources you need for your organization. They provide the partnership and collaboration to win larger engagements and they are the listening ear and voice of wisdom when you need a sounding board.

Strides for Success:

List 10 people who will support you in any way, personally or professionally.

Who do you know that will support your agenda and guide and mentor you? Who do you know that would help you with a business initiative? Who will partner with your organization to assure its success?

When I run executive events, the success of the event depends on its exposure and the value it brings to its participants. I am committed to providing highly valuable content and an amazing experience.

I could also use my own power base to support this initiative. The CEO of a bank that sponsors women's leadership and a number of community events is a phone call away, as is the business journal media contact I know who can help me promote the event in her business publications. I've built a relationship with a public relations firm that might brainstorm how to gain commercial visibility.

I have access to expert thought leaders in my circle of friends and colleagues who can speak at the event and know a restaurant who could cater the event and value being invited, as its exposure is a win-win for both of our organizations.

Who is only one or two calls away that could serve as your lifeline?

Now look at your list. How well do you know this person? A power base is a two-way street: You support them as much as they support you. Answer these questions:

What's the value he/she brings to you?

What are his/her business goals?

What are his/her personal goals and aspirations?

How would you describe his/her leadership communication style?

How would you rate this person's tolerance for risk?

What criteria does he/she focus on when making decisions?

What are his/her talents and gifts?

What are guaranteed ways to anger and frustrate him/her?

Who influences this person?

What are his/her personal interests?

It's been said that men are much better at developing their power base than woman. Perhaps as "givers" we are uncomfortable with taking. Instead look at developing a power base as using a skill you use naturally: developing empowering relationships, nurturing others while being nurtured yourself.

Develop your power base, and keep it alive and active, and you will see the effect it will have in your life, career, and business.

In summary, these are just a few of the tools used to Leverage leadership. Leaders who work to leverage their leadership by communicating powerfully, building a power base to support them, and by learning how to influence others experience less stress and overwhelm and build respectful collaborative relationships with others.

STEPPING FORWARD: IN SUMMARY, IN LEVERAGE YOU LEARNED:

1. How to communicate powerfully so your message is heard, understood, and acted upon.

2. The seven differing ways to influence and how to flex to the best communication strategy to enroll others in your ideas.

3. The value of having a power base and the key individuals who make up your power base support team.

Get your "Leverage" gifts at:

http://www.therenegadeleader.com/BookResources

This chapter was about the letter "L" for Leverage
in the L.E.A.D. Forward Formula™.

Next is "**E**" for Engage.

$\mathcal{E}$NGAGE: HOW TO MOVE PEOPLE TO PASSION, POSITIVITY, AND POSSIBILITY

5

I find leaders who lead teams ask the following questions:

- How can I get my people to do what I need them to do?

- What do I need to know to make sure I hire the right people?

- What can I do to bring out the best in my people, to build a strong team, and to manage effectively without sacrificing my life in the process?

The answer is Engage.

You learned how to Leverage your leadership in the previous chapter by communicating powerfully so your message is heard, understood, and acted upon, and how to build a power base and influence others by aligning your communication with their influence drivers. Now learn the strategies that engage and mobilize your team and organization to its highest performance.

The next step in the L.E.A.D. Forward Formula™ is "E" for Engage.

Jill: A Renegade in Heels

Jill seemed to manage it all as CEO of a consulting firm just outside Washington, DC. A well-dressed woman with an approachable personality, she spent her days managing her company and its staff, and personally meeting with others in her industry as well as her top clients to assure them of her dedication to their success. It was her dream to grow her company, to raise her children to be great leaders and citizens, and, post-divorce, to find a relationship that supported her both as a woman and as a CEO of a growing business.

Jill loved her clients and meeting their needs. However, as CEO, she was frustrated with managing the messier side of leadership: the people stuff. Yet she knew, in order to succeed, she needed to focus on strengthening relationships, engaging her people to high performance, developing behaviors for success, and maintaining a higher integrity of accountability. It wasn't easy managing new executive team leaders, engaging with virtual teams and building a unified culture with national employees.

That's when she brought in coaching to assist her in bridging the gap between her goals and her team's performance.

As her company began to expand, it became even more critical for Jill's message to be heard, not only by her customers and within her industry but also by her staff. Keeping her team highly functioning and accountable was key and trying to align a growing company to her vision required getting everyone on board and on the same page.

Once we worked together to build her plans for her company, Jill flew in her team for an executive retreat, and I joined her to facilitate the event. Our goal was to build consensus for attitudes, behaviors, and ways of communicating that were effective for the team and provided a consistency for clients. By the end of the day, the team had organized itself around 10 guiding principles. This built a foundation for their success, guiding their every decision, their team and organizational performance and creating a distinction for themselves in their industry.

Jill continued to expand her business and achieved recognition as the number-one reseller of her product/service in the nation.

Jill's business continues to evolve in the direction she wants it to go as her hallmark of excellent service and leadership remains the same. And her voice is heard in many ways: as a speaker, innovator, blogger, author, and renowned business leader.

SIDESTEPPING THE DRAMA

Jill's success strides included taking action; she realized that in order to be successful, she needed to pull her team together, to develop a shared vision, to determine the behaviors needed to achieve that vision, and to establish a trusting culture where every voice was heard. Her management team now had a common language of communication, accountability, actions, and goals. They were excited to be a part of the company, and the skills learned, the culture formed, and the goals agreed to became the foundation that supported organizational growth.

The new paradigm of leadership requires a skill set to engage today's workforce, spur creativity and innovation, and still be agile enough to flex with the continual waves of change. Each day you face a new Petri dish of complexity. Managing employees, virtual teams, and a global enterprise is more than challenging. People come to work each day with hearts, souls, minds, and loved ones to feed. It's up to you to get them excited to be there, to contribute their best work, and to promote innovation and creativity to assure the sustainability of business.

Engage means to move people to passion, positivity, and possibility. A new generation of employees, raised on the internet and within a collaborative culture, is turning its collective back on the ways of the past.

These new, modern employees are smarter, more innovative, more creative, and full of potential. But the old leadership model that's been around for generations doesn't address their needs—and as a result, that potential is going untapped.

And companies are suffering.

Employees are more disillusioned, disconnected, and disengaged than ever before. In fact, the 2013 Gallup Global Workplace Study reveals that in the United States just 29 percent of employees are engaged, coming to work each day ready to do what is expected of them, and Gallup estimates this as a loss in excess of $450 billion a year.

Your people want more than a paycheck for their work.

THE (DIS)ENGAGEMENT PROBLEM

The reason for all this workplace chaos? It's called disengagement.

An engaged employee is defined as one who arrives at work striving for excellence and focuses on the overall success of their employer. A disengaged employee is basically the opposite.

According to the U.S. results from the Towers Perrin's Global Workforce Study titled "Closing the Engagement Gap: A Roadmap for Driving Superior Business Performance," there is a direct link between employee engagement and business performance.

So if only 29 percent of employees are engaged, what are the others doing?

In a company of 100 employees, if only 29 show up daily feeling loyal to the company and committed to doing their best work over 70 are underperforming.

In addition, 77 of 100 employees report feeling burned out, 33 say they are overworked, 67 feel overwhelmed, 7 are sinking into deep depression, and 50 are open to switching jobs if another becomes available.

It doesn't paint a very pretty picture, does it?

And this disease is leading to the decline of many organizations.

There is accumulating evidence that corporations fail because their prevailing focus is on revenues, reducing costs, and improving operations. Of course, you recognize these functions as the arterial system of your organization, but what creates the pulse of the organization, feeds all of its roadways, and makes it sustainable?

The people who work for you.

Without commitment from your people, little success can be had, growth is difficult, and your competitors easily advance forward, leaving you in the dust.

The Conference Board on Employee Engagement reports that there is a direct correlation between employee engagement and desirable business outcomes such as retention of talent, customer service, individual performance, team performance, business unit productivity, and even enterprise-level financial performance.

That's why today's successful leaders, in addition to having a mission statement and a strategic plan, also develop a road map for the success and engagement of their people.

How to Engage & Mobilize People to Passion and Positivity

There are many simple strategies to engage and mobilize employees. They cost almost nothing to implement, can be put into place immediately, and have huge impact.

For instance, one opportunity that many leaders have—even in the C-suite—is to give more frequent, informal feedback about how each employee is doing. That way, everyone in an organization knows what is expected of them and how they can continue to grow, learn, and improve.

Strides for Success:

In coaching we build an "engage and mobilize" plan with our clients. We help you measure and understand the pulse of engagement for your organization, for your team. In addition to using resources such as the Gallup Q12 Employee Engagement survey and customized assessments, here are seven simple questions every leader can ask of his/her employees:

1. Do you know what is expected of you, in your role, on your team, by the organization?

2. What do you feel you are doing successfully?

3. What, if anything, would help you to feel more successful at the end of the day?

4. How can we help you to get there?

5. (If appropriate): What will happen if you improve (e.g., more responsibility, more time with leadership, more desirable assignments)?

6. (If appropriate): What will happen if you don't overcome this barrier?

7. How can I help?

While all of these questions are important, the last question is especially important. It shows the employee that you care and are committed to his/her success.

The biggest complaint I hear from employees is that they don't know where they stand with their managers, as they receive little or no feedback until performance review time. Instead, keep the conversation about performance ongoing. Know that as a leader you role is to know and grow your employees.

HOW TO CLIMB MOUNT EVEREST—IN HEELS

More than ever, we are learning that the more women leaders stay true to who they really are, the easier their team will be to lead.

Katherine Krug, COO of an app company called Everest, suggests that women get further and move faster on their career path when they focus on what makes them good leaders. For women, she says that means tapping into your natural ability to connect with others and not focusing on how *you* are going to stay competitive, but how *your team* is going to stay competitive.

It's no secret that women select their shoes based on their outfit or the need for comfort, or they simply choose the shoes that will take them through the terrain of that day. Katherine says the best women CEOs and leaders are the ones who use those inherent skills and qualities to become one with their teams, not the ones who run ahead of them. In other words, spend the same amount of consideration when analyzing the individual strengths of your team members as you do your shoes. Just as you select the right shoe for the job, allow your people to be in the work role designed for their talents. This way, you can find the shoe that best fits their needs and ultimately optimize their results, rather than going about it the other way around.

Katherine told *Forbes* magazine that this approach works better for women in business because it takes out the "stress" we associate with needing to maintain that competitive edge at the head of the conference table. It also takes the stress off the employees when it comes to performance, because they know that you have taken the time to match them with the jobs that they will do best. They relax more and feel more equipped and prepared to do their job, and, even better, they *want* to do their jobs.

It's a strategy that works far better than giving people a task they can't do, and then having everyone start from scratch all over again, more stressed and under more pressure than when they started the job in the first place.

The result is a win-win for everyone, and it's a way that women leaders today are stepping ahead of their male counterparts in the C-suite, in just the right pair of shoes.

Mindy Grossman, CEO of HSN Inc. since 2006, has focused on leading her team with equal success. An "engaged culture" was her top priority when she came on board, and it had to be since she was the umpteenth CEO to take the chair in a very short amount of time. Employee faith was low, and her mission, which she chose to accept, was to strap on some work shoes and get down to business.

Since Mindy came on board, employee morale has increased exponentially, all due to the multi-pronged platform she developed in order to create the engaged culture the company desperately needed.

There are few (if any) employees with HSN who do not understand the vision and goals for the company that Mindy has set forward. She initiated her vision and keeps it clear and focused through a dedicated company intranet system the team uses to ensure transparent communication. In addition to this, she holds town hall meetings with the team every eight weeks to keep her fingers on the pulse of any key points.

And that's not all.

If you work at HSN and are celebrating your fifth, 10th, 15th, 20th, or 25th anniversary with the company, Mindy will sit down and have lunch with you. Why? She wants to know what makes you, someone who has an established personal record of loyalty and commitment, enjoy working at the same company she does.

Mindy isn't the only woman executive who believes that employees need to be treated above and beyond the standard Corporate America is current providing. Despite the economic climate, high-quality employees today know their worth and won't stay with a company that doesn't recognize it. The most successful women visionaries in business have gotten to where they are today because they know their value, and if their employer doesn't recognize it, they move on to a company that does.

Now, these same visionaries are taking the concept that got them to this point in their careers, and running with it—paying it forward to each and every one of their team members.

Katherine Krug reached the top of *Everest* by engaging her employee culture. She's not one of those leaders and visionaries to focus only on her own success, because she knows her company will do well when each of her employees does well. In fact, the company Everest is aptly named, because one of the company visions is to push each and every one of their employees to the absolute limit, personally and professionally. Everest is dedicated to helping their employees pursue their dreams.

In a recent year, Katherine helped each of her executives realize a personal goal that would help them grow. One received DJ lessons so that he could pursue a disco business on the side; another received an around-the-world airline ticket so he could visit 30 countries before his 30th birthday. A third got a health coach so that he could begin the fitness regime he desperately needed.

None of these things directly produced profit for the company—if anything, they cost the company money—but it was an investment that Katherine made, and continues to make, because she knows that a valuable employee is a loyal, highly productive, and engaged employee, and that in the long term will provide a much greater return on her investment.

What is your strategy to engage?

To engage and mobilize, begin by looking at the unique needs of each of your team members and determine how to align their needs with what we know to be the top employee engagement drivers.

GIVE YOUR PEOPLE WHAT THEY WANT

So what does it take to engage your workforce? The 2013 Employee Engagement report provides a brief overview of engagement levels worldwide, focusing on the engagement-retention connection, key drivers, and the ways that the behavior of managers and senior leaders influence engagement. It also explores the specific roles and responsibilities of the workforce in building a more engaged organization.

In order to activate employee engagement, the report indicates that employees need to know what they want—and what the organization needs—and then take action to achieve both. Managers can build rapport with employees by activating coaching skills to build strong relationships and dialogue so that they understand each person's talents, interests, and needs, and match those with the organizational objectives. Lastly, executives can promote higher levels of engagement by having a demonstrated consistency in words and actions to align employees to the organizational goals.

Strides for Success:

The Towers Perrin's Global Workforce Study, like the majority of the latest employee engagement studies, indicates that there are 10 drivers of employee engagement that impact business results.

Look at the list below and assess how well you, your organization, and your employees rate in these key areas:

1. Senior management's sincere interest in employee well-being

2. Opportunities to improve skills and capabilities

3. The organization's reputation for social responsibility

4. Opportunities to provide input into decision-making in the employee's department

5. The organization's ability to quickly resolve customer concerns

6. An individual employee's own readiness to set high personal standards

7. Excellent career advancement opportunities

8. An individual employee's interest in challenging work assignments

9. Employees' relationship with supervisors

10. The organization's willingness to encourage innovative thinking

These key areas are characteristics of a "people-centered" style of management.

The effects that people-centered leadership can have on your bottom line are eye-opening. Performance isn't the only thing that soars; profits also soar. With increased engagement, teams function better, tasks are performed with ease, little time is wasted, and there is greater commitment to improving the bottom line in all areas.

The research also shows that women have the ideal leadership attributes to meet the employee engagement challenge. Use what comes naturally to engage your people, and to build strong teams and a high-performance organization fueled by passion and positivity. I refer to it as the ABCs of leadership.

To be effective you:

A: Align others to the big vision.

B: Build the behaviors needed to achieve that vision.

C: Create a culture of collaboration, where everyone has a voice and can impact in the decisions that affect their work.

Here's how to get started.

Know Your Team

Walk in the shoes of your team members. Visualize a person on your team. Ask yourself the following questions:

What are their career aspirations?

What are their personal aspirations?

What motivates them?

What are their values?

What are their talents, gifts, and skills?

What is their primary communication style?

What are their professional development needs?

How well are you able to answer these questions for every member of your team?

Messages that Inspire and Mobilize

Communicating to motivate is important, too. Below are samplings of motivating messages:

- Here is where we have been....

- Here is where we are going....

- Here is why what we are doing matters and how what you are doing matters....

- Here are our values and what we stand for....

- Here are our top strategies and initiatives, and here is how your role fits in....

- Here are our top objectives/performance indicators, as well as yours, and how they fit in....

- Here is your specific role, and how it connects to our vision, mission, and strategy....

- What support do you need from me?

In summary, Engage, like Leverage, is a verb. It requires action. Building an employee engagement plan is your first step.

How to Get Everyone on the Same Page

Another strategy to Engage is by gaining the consensus of others around you. We use a tool called the Leadership Dashboard. In common language we talk about "getting everyone on the same page." When I worked with Nicole this what we started with—self-identifying what would be most important to every member of the executive leadership team—so when she presented she would meet the needs of both the team and the individuals on the team. Once teams and organizations have shared values and goals it is easy to make decisions.

"We don't have a shared way of making decisions," A client recently said hesitantly in our coaching call. "We are not on the same page." And isn't this a common statement you hear again and again? Are you ever baffled by the decisions that are made at the top or the work that is being done that doesn't match the goals you set out to accomplish? Do you cry in your pillow at night with disbelief that someone within your organization would treat your customer with less than your idea of customer service excellence?

It is because you are not on the same page. Something magical happens when you lead from shared values and use the same filter to make all decisions. The executive retreats I lead are often packed with critical decisions that need to be made, problems to be solved, initiatives to be approved. Because each team member is "on the same page" we breeze through the agenda, leaving the meeting early, feeling refreshed, and having enough time for an informal lunch together.

Imagine spending half of your time in meetings. Imagine everyone offering ideas that aligned with the goals. Imagine leaving a meeting invigorated instead of exhausted and overwhelmed.

That is what happens when you have a methodology for building your unique shared leadership dashboard. It's a treasure map to success. Each decision is made using the same lens, factoring business success, employees, and consumers, and stakeholders into every choice. And in Renegade style, I recommend leaving room for innovation, stretch, and possibility.

Having a Leadership Dashboard:

- Results in more strategic decision-making.

- Minimizes room for costly mistakes.

- Creates quicker resolution.

- Honors the values and goals the organization maintains.

- Gets you out of meetings and spending your time on what is most impactful.

The Leadership Dashboard is a simple one-page tool that summarizes the most important things to focus on, at least for the moment! Is your team on the "same page"?

Use the questions below to see if your team members offer similar responses.

- The organization's vision, where are we going?

- The organization's purpose and mission, why are we here?

- Values, what is our shared foundation of values?

- Strategic edge, what sets us apart from others?

- Our top three initiatives, what are they?

- Name our key performance indicators to track success?

- What relationships do we need to build that will foster support of our goals?

- What are our top strategies to build organizational capacity?

You can also create a career/professional dashboard covering the same areas, assessing the alignment between the organization's direction or not, and how to take the steps to close any gaps. Perhaps most importantly, everyone in the organization can create their own dashboard. When this exercise is done properly, everyone is aligned, focused on what matters, and accountable. Each dashboard rolls up into the larger whole—using only a single sheet of paper!

The process is extraordinary because it is so simple, practical, and powerful. In today's world of super-complicated algorithms, virtual communication, and gut-wrenching volatility, it is refreshing to have a tool like the Leadership Dashboard to keep us all "on the same page."

HOW TO BUILD HIGH-PERFORMANCE TEAMS

You can plan for success, build an employee engagement plan, and get everyone on the same page with the Leadership Dashboard, but it is up to your people to decide if they are willing to perform. You can't demand performance these days; you can't coerce people into doing what you want.

Building effective teams is hard. Many employees, even at senior levels, lack the ability to build and participate on teams effectively.

Interpersonal dynamics create lots of friction and hassles that are time consuming and challenging to overcome. It is rare for team members to know how to set expectations and create engagement in ways that get great results while strengthening relationships.

So much is said about having a high-performance team, but what does that look like, and how does one develop one?

The secret is you don't. You lead them to become a high-performing team, but it is the team who becomes inspired to take action and as a result outperforms expectations. When teams perform they engage in open, honest communication, strengthen relationships, improve productivity, and move the team toward results. As a woman you can do this with ease.

In coaching we use a team assessment or a change management personality assessment to understand the change capacity of a team followed by a 15-step framework to identify where the team is now and the goals and objectives of the team. From there we build a navigation plan. I have found that when the leader demonstrates high performance the team follows.

Strides for Success:

Team Assessment: Are team members going for the same goal?

Have you ever had a conversation with a friend only to discover you were both talking about different topics? Teams have the same concern. One team member might be talking about vision, while another is wondering about specific initiatives, another is focused on evaluating ideas, and still another is frustrated that no one is committing to specific action steps. In addition, some team members aren't saying anything at all or are making negative comments.

The next time you have a team meeting, write down the names of the team members across this page. Every time someone speaks, check off what kind of conversation they are having. Then you can see whether your team is truly aligned and on the same page, or moving in different directions. You can also see who is dominating the conversation (often the most vocal is the one to lead a team down the wrong path) and who is disengaged. Soon you might also start to recognize what it important to each team member. A visionary needs to know the direction you are taking. A coach personality needs to know how this idea will impact your customers; another might need to know the return on investment etc.

Develop a Shared Language to Navigate Change, Launch Big Ideas, and Solve Problems

Imagine having a shared way of conversing that maximizes the time you spend in meeting, shifts the focus from what is wrong to what is possible, and builds your road map for accountability?

Use this simple IGNITE™ framework to engage your team into designing a shared plan for moving forward. Use this simple script for your next meeting, to give feedback, or to present a new idea. I've known clients who tell me they keep the IGNITE™ script in their pocketbook to walk them through necessary conversations. Use IGNITE™ with your team to engage them in the desired outcomes.

- **Illuminate:** Put the spotlight on what the situation is now; describe it.

- **Generate:** Share the vision, goal, or objective; define the destination.

- **Navigate:** Determine how to get where you are and where you/ and your teams want to be; develop the road map, together.

- **I**ntegrate: Combine actions, words, and behavior to achieve the desired outcome; define the mile markers along the way and set the metrics and time frame for success.

- **T**ranslate: Translate the result; identify why this process/idea is taking place and agree how you will know when you are successful.

- **E**valuate: Celebrate your results and decide what you'll tackle next! Take the time to review what you did right and what you can course-correct for the next adventure.

Use the IGNITE™ framework and your meetings will come alive with collaboration, creativity, engagement, and commitment.

Use Words that Motivate and Promote Accountability

Employees tell us managers give a poor instruction, which causes misunderstandings, wasted time, and wasted energy, and leads to frustration and resentment.

They feel ill-informed about what is happening in the company and often confused about what the company is trying to achieve.

It is an old saying but one worth repeating at this point: In order to be understood we must first understand. You've learned how to get everyone on the same page with the Leadership Dashboard and using the IGNITE Framework™ to move your team to high performance. Now let's add in accountability.

Want to know the one sentence you can use that will transform accountability, provide clear communication, and release the pressure cooker of stress you experience each and every day? This one sentence offers a 100-percent guaranteed return in all of my clients, and now I'm going to gift it to you:

"*Who* will do *what* by *when*—and *how* will I know?"

Use it in every meeting and every conversation, and you'll find your teams giving you the answer long before you ask the question.

When you understand what engages and motivate your team, you begin to communicate in a way that promotes positivity and possibility. Every team member feels valued, every voice is heard, and those who participate in creating a navigation plan tend to stick with the road map. Sidestep your inner nurturer and worry about accountability; create the shared language of values and use the sentence "who will do what by when—and how will I know?" to embrace a common language of accountability. You will feel relieved, your people will perform better, and with deep engagement the change in the office atmosphere will be palpable.

STEPPING FORWARD: IN SUMMARY, IN ENGAGE YOU:

1. Learned the challenges that most leaders face due to low employee engagement.

2. Learned ways to use communication to Engage, mobilize, and inspire your teams.

3. Discovered the IGNITE™ script to use in a one-on-one conversation or with your team or organization.

4. Were introduced to the concept of building guiding principles of shared values, behaviors, and objectives.

5. Were given an exercise to begin your Leadership Dashboard and to activate maximum engagement from each individual while creating a high-production teams.

Get your "Engage" gifts at:

http://www.therenegadeleader.com/BookResources

This was the letter "E" for Engage in the
L.E.A.D. Forward Formula™.

Next is "**A**" for Activate.

6 ACTIVATE: A CULTURE OF COLLABORATION AND INNOVATION

The L.E.A.D. Forward Formula™ has helped you discover how to Leverage your authentic leadership style so you portray a powerful leadership presence. Success does not happen in a vacuum; it is birthed with other people. Next you learned how to Engage and mobilize for high performance. Now let's take that to its highest level and learn how to Activate a culture of positivity and possibility.

We know that in order to survive business requires rethinking, reinvention, and reimagining what is possible. Organizations like Apple, Starbucks, and Google are forever in a state of change. Now let's look at the role of leadership in the tallest heels of management.

ELEVATING YOUR LEADERSHIP: THE VIEW FROM THE TOP

Instead of leading a team, you're in charge of an entire organization. You are responsible for increasing revenues, achieving effectiveness and efficiencies in all operations, cutting costs without reducing quality, and being compliant with government and industry regulations. In addition to achieving bottom-line results or positioning the company as a contender in their industry, the questions I hear at this level include:

- Will my company continue to succeed, or will something happen that will mean I lose everything and fail?

- How will I manage all of these relationships with the board, stakeholders, employees, and political and industry leaders?

- How can I be seen as a successful leader, have my own powerful voice be heard, and be respected a leader?

- Who can I turn to for help when I'm the one who's supposed to have all the answers?

To stay relevant, how do you lead an organization and activate a culture the nurtures and sustains every seedling of hope, inspiration, and idea, and continues to spur creativity and innovation in the hearts and minds of its people?

Meet Wendy Tirollo,
CEO of TRM Microwave

"I joined TRM in 1994. One of the first projects I worked on was ISO certification, which wasn't easy but offered a great learning challenge. In 1996 I was promoted to human resources, where I remained for 10 years. This gave me great insight to people and their motivations, and it was important to me that everyone was happy to work here.

"In 2006, the owner asked if I would consider moving into senior management. My first reaction was that I had to think about it. Having the lives of employees hanging in the balance due to the decisions made by senior management seemed daunting. Many of the employees had been with us for years and I would be responsible for keeping the company thriving to support them. I also worried that given my conservative nature, I wouldn't be able to make the hard decisions. And I also secretly worried that since I was not an engineer, would what I knew be enough?

"I moved into senior management and advanced as CEO in 2010.

"My first challenge in leading an organization was in being taken seriously in meetings or in direct face-to-face communications. Somehow, requests made in my quiet soft voice were misunderstood as 'nice to have' instead of a directive. I had to work on finding my power voice and asserting myself a bit more.

"I also struggled with being a perfectionist, which would take me too deeply into the details. I had to train myself to focus on the big picture. I wasn't going to change my persona or how I spoke; I simply had to find the management style that worked for me.

"Focusing on culture is important. Working in HR helped me to deal with people of all personalities. Approaching each person appropriately is an important skill. I read and continue to learn. I've learned about how important employee morale is, and how it affects productivity. It's always on my radar screen.

"Because we focus on having a family-like culture, our employees treat our business like it is their own. We all have a fire in our belly to succeed and we grade ourselves on a monthly basis for all to see. We meet our goals.

"We treat our customers with the same degree of excellence, taking on the jobs that seem too unique to provide. We do what others don't quite successfully, and have built a brand around our ability to do so.

"My advice to leaders of organizations is to make sure your employees get what they need and are happy. We empower them to get what they need to feel successful at the end of the day. Also have great people on your team. I meet with my executive team weekly and we also hold quarterly off-site meetings. I stick my nose in every department, just to keep in touch. I have lunch with my teams to get to know them—and they know when I am coming, due to the sound of my own high heels!"

As you read the advice of women CEOs, you're likely noticing that the real work begins at the top. You're the boss. You're a leader. And suddenly you realize…maybe success isn't exactly what you thought it would be. Not that you're complaining. You're thankful to be where you are and grateful to anyone and everyone who helped you get there. And even more, you're proud of yourself—of everything you've learned and accomplished and sacrificed along the way to get where you are today.

You deserve it. But still, sometimes you can't help thinking, "When do I get to the fun part?" That's the question most of my clients ask. That's the dirty little secret about making it to the top. The climb can be a lot more fun than the arrival. Before you even have time to catch your breath, or adjust to the altitude, or take in the view, another, bigger mountain of problems that need solving and questions that need answering pops up right in front of you.

You are the leader others will either choose to follow, or not. One way to gain followers is by being interesting, allowing others to know you personally and professionally. We begin by building your platform and that of your organization so that your employees and industry truly understand what you stand for. When you build a high-performance culture you gain:

Higher productivity.

Better teamwork.

Improved alignment throughout the organization.

Great respect for the leadership team.

An organization that lives by its mission and values.

LEADING FROM THE CORNER OFFICE: CREATING A SUCCESSFUL ORGANIZATIONAL CULTURE

Most leaders review their culture constantly, standing on the sidelines and looking out into their organization. You look at the organization's structure, its success, its challenges, its partner relationships, its fiscal strength. As you look onto your culture's horizons ask these questions:

Why are you dissatisfied with the current culture?

Which parts of the culture are not satisfactory and why?

What are examples you give?

What parts of the culture work?

And what are examples of specific situations when the culture is working?

Define the culture. What do you want it to be?

What becomes possible for your organization when the culture changes?

And what becomes possible for you personally?

After years of research and positive client results, I published the I.N.F.L.U.E.N.C.E. Framework™ in *The Renegade Leader: 9 Success Strategies Driven Leaders Use to Influence People, Ignite Performance and Impact Profits*. Founded upon proven employee engagement strategies, psychology, and neuroscience principles, the framework offers actions you can take to reignite the passion in your people, create a culture of collaboration, and achieve overall high performance. Culture requires constant attention and ongoing evaluation.

The Renegade Leader devotes one chapter to each letter of the acronym I.N.F.L.U.E.N.C.E. while engaging you in the fable of a CEO facing the challenges of a merger, low employee engagement, and trying to evolve leadership skills within the organization. Each chapter demonstrates the implementation of the framework. As a result, the business prospers and the CEO also creates an organization that has inspired leadership, is built upon a foundation of trust, fosters leadership at all levels, and listen and tunes into its employees, customers, investors, and vendors. Its culture unleashes the full potential in its people, invokes collaboration through transparent communication, and develops a new respect for the brilliance of each individual.

Below you will find a brief introduction to the I.N.F.L.U.E.N.C.E. Framework™.

Inspired Leadership: Creating the Spark

Inspire high performance and innovation by being an inspired leader.

Nourish Trust: Gaining Sure-Footed Traction in Your Organization

Build a trusting culture by establishing guiding principles of behavior.

Foster Leadership at All Levels: Embracing the Highest Standards

Delegate with clear direction and inspire leadership in all by building a learning organization and showing confidence in others' abilities.

Listen to Quiet or Unfamiliar Voices: Tuning into the Patter of Other Feet

Ask powerful coaching questions to promote engagement and invite communication at all levels.

Unleash the Potential in Your People

Give others permission to be brilliant.

Engage in Transparent Communication

Implement systems that allow employees to voice their ideas at all levels and to keep informed of the organizational goals.

Notice and Recognize Achievement

Communicate praise for high performance and for failing forward.

Create a Culture of Collaboration

Build strong teams by creating focused groups and think tanks; share decision-making responsibility.

Enjoy and Respect Diversity: Developing Cultural Intelligence

Value the richness of diversity and embrace the uniqueness of each person's contribution.

After reviewing this framework and the current research, it is clear to see why, as a woman, you are best equipped to lead today's organizations. Empathy, connection, inclusion, and open communication contribute to creating an organization based upon a foundation of trust, commitment, and values.

Tara: A Renegade in Heels

Tara's company had been in business for more than 20 years. By any measure, it was successful—seven locations, nearly 500 employees—yet Tara knew something was missing. As a part owner, she wanted to own the company solo to have a greater impact, to develop it into what she thought possible, which included growth and expansion as opposed to maintaining the company's current position.

Tara saw potential for the company to be a significant leader in its industry—with the systems of a big company yet the entrepreneurial spirit of a startup. She knew the company culture needed something, but just wasn't sure what it was. With coaching, her goals were: 1) negotiating and acquiring the company; 2) pulling the culture together; and 3) expanding the organization.

Loving the desire of a driven leader, I was readily on board. I helped her present, negotiate, and ultimately purchase the main ownership of the company. Next, I looked over the horizon of the company. As is the case in many businesses, good employees had been promoted into management but weren't given the management and leadership skills needed to keep others accountable, to assume roles of fiscal responsibility, and to keep a vision alive and active with their teams.

I also noticed that there wasn't a consistent means of communication among the seven locations; each location was its own silo, consistent in operation but disconnected in communication. Tara wanted that family feel—that sense of being cared about that they offered to their clients brought in-house.

Our work started with a management survey to understand the level of employee engagement and satisfaction within the company and to assess the leadership skill set. Tara was surprised to learn that many managers struggled with communication skills, providing feedback, inspiring others to do their best, and holding the line on accountability. They also expressed concern about the organization growth plan. Where are we going as a company? Reacting to change, positive or negative; they were worried and resistance was raising its head.

When asked about the goals of the organization, myriad responses came back, without a consistent message. We agreed that the company would not be able to grow without their people engaged, on board, and positioned for growth.

I designed a customized leadership training program that would help the managers understand the key drivers of employee engagement, and give them the communication and coaching skills to lead and mentor others, and to design, together, the ideal organizational culture that could position the company for growth.

Training doesn't build leadership muscle unless it is used over and over again. Leaders have questions: *How do I use what I learned with my team? How do I use it to meet my department goals? What do I do if I have questions?*

To serve these needs we worked with the managers and their teams post training. We began with a team performance assessment, and worked together to not only implement the new learning but to build a stronger team with clear objectives.

As a result, we fostered engagement and leadership at every level: supervisor, manager, team, all the way down to the employees.

Once leadership activated their 21st-century skill sets, together looked at the culture. There wasn't a consistent answer to "who are we, what do we stand for, how are we different than our competitors?"

I believe in co-creation so with the executive team we designed and I facilitated Culture Day, a manager and executive team retreat. We determined what had made the company so successful for Over two decades and narrowed this knowledge down to five key words. We then identified the behaviors that represented those key words and discussed how to hold others accountable for those behaviors, how to hire for those behaviors, and how to assess for them at performance reviews.

Each team then took on a particular goal within their organization and I worked with each facility to achieve it. By now the shift was starting to happen. Employees were engaged, and managers were more productive and feeling valued for being part of the discussions. The CEO engaged in transparent communication to promote further engagement and to show a genuine interest in employees.

In summary their culture was driven by shared values. Those values became their table of success, and everyone knew how to own their seat. Transparent communication was achieved by establishing an in-house social media portal where all managers and teams could talk about decisions affecting their work, share innovative ideas, and create focus groups to tackle hot topics. This company implemented all aspects of the I.N.F.L.U.E.N.C.E. Framework™, resulting in a unified culture of engaged people whose great performance contributed to the organization's growth, positioning for expansion, and long-term sustainability.

Over time we achieved the following results:

The company surpassed its financial goals, growing by six times the national average for its industry and achieving record profitability, all within a turbulent economy.

While others in their industry were closing their doors, they opened a new location and hired 100 new employees. Within 18 months, that location was as prosperous as the rest.

The company was awarded Business of the Year in 2013 and its CFO was recognized as one of the top financial officers as well. Tara became a recognized voice in her industry, serving on the national board and having the time to share a political voice representing the impact of new healthcare laws and other concerns in their industry.

The organization, solid in its future with a growth plan to more than triple in size within eight years, also established a non-profit organization, solidifying its commitment to give back to the community.

With the managers able to lead effectively, the executive team was now free to engage in innovative thinking and take action on expanding the business.

STEPS IN SHIFTING CULTURE

Why do we need to activate a shift in culture? You focus on culture when your organization is impacted by change and also to stay relevant.

A sample of change events includes:

New senior management.

A new product or service launch.

Mergers or acquisitions.

A recognized need for higher performance.

Promoting collaboration and innovation.

Managing a change initiative without resistance.

Competitively positioning the organization.

Growing the organization.

Changing behaviors.

Rallying around a new brand.

Shifting from a bureaucratic to an entrepreneurial culture.

And so many more.

With organizations in a constant flux of change, ask yourself if your culture supports or challenges your goals. If it is not in alignment, take the steps to shift!

Strides for Success:

Look at your culture and see if it is alignment for your success and the goals of your organization.

Evaluate if it's time to bring your culture and its leaders into the evolved 21st century. Does your culture offer opportunities for innovative ideas to be shared? Is there trust or cracks in your trust foundation? Are your people able to give you the information you need to make the decisions that are most impactful, or better yet, have you provided them with a way to do so?

Have all of your leaders been given the skills they need to succeed?

Are your teams positioned to be agile during change? We assess for change management personalities to assure that you have the right mix of people on your teams and in your organizations. Do you lead with your head (vision) heart (people) or hands (task)? What personality mix are your teams? We have found teams of 15 visionaries, three coaches, and one executer, no wonder the process of change was not getting done!

What are your culture's performance, values, and behaviors? What do you want them to be? What attitudes, behaviors, beliefs, and actions would you need to see to know the change in culture was successful?

Culture change does not occur over night but the subtle changes can have a big impact. Activating a cultural change is like dating: You begin with one relationship and work on all of the rest (relatives) before the marriage.

Make the activation measurable. Know your point A and your point B. Communicate openly with your employees and, most importantly, know and share your "why." With any change every person wants to know the "why."

Lastly, celebrate the small wins. So many organizations set their eyes on the big goal and fail to keep up the momentum by recognizing the smaller steps along the way.

Personally I love to work with culture. The results are very impactful, the work stimulating, and coaching is provided at all levels, broad and deep, supporting the organization's success at every tier. As you walk the halls note the culture as it is now and envision what might be possible.

THE I.N.F.L.U.E.N.C.E. FRAMEWORK™: WEAR THE SHOES OTHERS CHOOSE TO FOLLOW

Below you will find actions you can take to look at your culture with a new lens and position it for the future.

How to Inspire Innovation: Creating an Inspired Organization:

"I had no idea that being your authentic self could make me as rich as I've become. If I had, I'd have done it a lot earlier."

~ Oprah Winfrey

1. **Get inspired yourself.**

   ❖ Maintain your health, spirit, and drive.

   ❖ Be committed to achieving your results.

   ❖ Be clear about your vision for the organization.

2. **Focus on people before tasks.**

   ❖ Discover the unique strengths, talents, passions, and values of your employees, and find ways that allow them to use this brilliance in their job functions.

   ❖ Ask them what they need to feel successful at the end of the day, and help them to create the work, learning opportunities, and growth that meet those objectives.

3. **Share the big vision.**

   ❖ Your people are ready for it. It's far from motivating to only see a small part of a big picture. If you're excited, your people will be, too. Let them be part of setting the course for success. They will be much more committed to a plan of action that they helped to create.

4. Let your people know you value their contribution.

It's disempowering to make a widget on an assembly line without knowing how it fits into the product it helps to produce.

5. Manage with visibility and emotional connection.

❖ Don't be afraid to be present—to show up fully—even when you don't know the answers or times are difficult.

❖ You inspire others when you show them you are confident in them, yourself, and your organization to meet the challenges that arise.

6. Model for others what you expect of them.

❖ Be an example by living the values you want your organization to exude. If you don't want to waste time on gossip, for example, don't talk about others. If you want people to arrive to meetings on time, don't be late yourself. If you want employees to trust you and be open, allow them space to be heard.

❖ Increase your capacity for empathy, listening, and emotional and social intelligence.

7. Self-monitor your own energy.

❖ Everyone experiences highs and lows. Know that as a leader, your lows affect the people around you, at work as well as at home. Develop a strategy to shake off the lows, put negative energy aside, and move forward through these periods. Not only will your people be positively impacted, but you will experience improved health and peace of mind (and so will your family!).

8. **Use powerful words to inspire powerful change.**

    ❖ Examples include: "reveal," "validate," "motivate," "compel,"
    "elaborate," "assure," "emphasize," "action," "entice," "gain,"
    "optimize," and "leverage."

How to Become a Trustworthy Leader: Building a Culture of High Trust

> *"The fastest way to create cultural change is to start acting the
> way you wish the company would start to act, and very soon it
> starts to catch on."*
>
> ~ Irene B. Rosenfeld, CEO, Mondelez International

As I was researching this book, I heard over and over that it is difficult as a woman to establish trust, both with men and with the women below you. Many surveyed said they distrust women superiors as they feel some women can hold them back, requiring them to work harder to advance and to prove themselves before being promoted.

The reality is this: All leaders need to pay attention to trust. Simple cracks in your trust foundation will not only cause you to trip and fall, they will prevent your goals from moving forward.

Do you experience any of these conditions in your organization?

- Resistance to change
- Sabotage and hiding behaviors
- Negative attitudes
- Finger-pointing and lack of accountability
- Complaining and focusing on problems instead of solutions

These are all examples of cracks in your trust foundation. However, the good news is trust can be rebuilt. The best ways to build trust are to be credible, and to be authentic and consistent in your leadership. When people know their leader is predictable, they respond better. Adapt the characteristics below to establish trust up, down, and sideways.

Characteristics of trustworthy managers include:

- Integrity.

- Reliability.

- Caring.

- Openness.

- Competence.

- Loyalty.

- Fairness.

As Stephen M.R. Covey, author of *Speed of Trust*, stated, trust between people can be built rather quickly but it can all evaporate into thin air if it becomes threatened in the slightest way. Like a rosebud, trust must be fed, nourished, and led to develop and grow independently on its own. The most influential leaders in the world know this, and nourish their people daily.

Nourishing Trust: Build from the Ground Up

1. **Make a commitment to yourself and your team to be credible and authentic.**

   ❖ Become the leader you were meant to be, not a copy of somebody else.

2. **Be reliable and of high integrity.**

   ❖ Never make an agreement that you don't fully intend to keep, no matter how small.

   ❖ If you ever fall short of meeting a deadline or agreement, apologize immediately to everyone involved.

3. **Be clear about everyone's roles and responsibilities.**

   ❖ Stay fair without favoritism.

   ❖ Never dismiss one person while engaging others.

4. **Notice how you react to changes.**

   ❖ Unpredictability in behavior feeds distrust. If you blow up or appear unable to handle difficulties calmly, staff members will become trained to hide problems until they escalate. Their fears may keep them frozen in place, not knowing the right action to take but unwilling to risk dealing with your anger and judgment.

5. **Be committed to your core values and the principles and values of your organization.**

   ❖ "Walk the talk."

Foster Leadership in Others: Encourage Teamwork and Collaboration

"My key role is to continue to develop future leaders."
~ Debra L. Reed, CEO, Sempra Energy

Leah Busque, CEO of TaskRabbit and former IBM engineer, says, *"I wake up every morning and think to myself, how far can I push the company forward in the next 24 hours?"*

How to Foster Leadership in Others

1. **Ask powerful questions.**

    ❖ Others can't lead if you don't invite them in. Ask for their opinions, ideas, and concerns.

2. **Create focus groups, although I prefer to call them "transformation teams."**

    If you have an idea or problem you would like to resolve, put these transformation teams into the driver's seat, asking them to analyze and determine the next step to bring the idea to fruition or correct the situation. What idea can you bring to the next team meeting?

3. **Establish your shared decision-making values.**

    ❖ In *Delivering Happiness*, Zappos CEO Tony Hsieh discusses the company's core values, upon which every decision is made—values such as "Deliver Wow through service," "Do more with less," and "Create fun and little weirdness." What are yours?

    ❖ Another organization uses three-legged stool guidelines for every decision, asking, "Does it benefit employees, the customer, and the organization?" If any of these fail, the decision is no. All three legs are needed for support; if one should weaken or break, the whole stool tumbles. What are your key decision-making values?

    ❖ When you establish shared decision-making criteria, everyone is able to make decisions using the same filter.

4. **Work with your team to establish guiding principles of behavior.**

    ❖ One client referred to this as "10 Golden Rules." In order to adhere to your standards of excellence, what behaviors must be demonstrated daily? Remember that leadership is modeled. Employees don't know how to be leaders unless they are shown how to lead. Recognize those who follow your guiding principles and soon you will have an entire team of leaders.

5. **Train your people, and bring leadership to all levels.**

   ❖ Recent studies show that leaders who have coaching skills create more than a 30-percent increase in performance compared to those leaders who lack that competency. Help your managers learn how to coach their teams more effectively as well.

6. **Bring the topic of leadership into the room.**

   ❖ Define what the word "leader" means within your organization. Talk about what attributes make great leadership and what behaviors model that effectively.

7. **Set expectations for leadership.**

   ❖ Expect others to be willing to be in the spotlight. Share the leadership runway with others who want to model their best competencies!

Listening to the Quiet Voices

"I think the one lesson I have learned is that there is no substitute for paying attention."

~ Diane Sawyer, ABC News Anchor

As a leader it is easy to give attention to the helpful few—the ones who speak up, who volunteer, who take charge in a meeting. But what about the others? What about the quiet ones—the ones who need a little time to process before sharing their ideas or the ones who need to be invited to feel safe enough to speak? A key part of leadership is to appreciate differences; not everyone wears the same shoes. So how do you invite others to join you on the runway?

1. **Ask, ask, and ask again until your employees understand that you really want their input.**

    ❖ What do you think?

    ❖ If this was your project, what would you do?

    ❖ Where would you start?

    ❖ What would be the value to the company in doing this?

    ❖ How does this feel to you?

    ❖ How would this affect our people, our operation, our customers, and our bottom line?

2. **Listen deeply for what is not said.**

    ❖ Is this person very attached to the outcome?

    ❖ What emotion is the person expressing?

3. **Listen without reacting to differing perspectives.**

    ❖ To be an inspired and inspiring leader, leave your judgment robe on the hook by the front door.

    ❖ Calmly take the idea and, like a prism, hold it in the light, turning it all around to see every facet. See what is possible from all sides.

    ❖ Ask powerful questions and come to a joint conclusion. When you provide your team with all the information you have, more often than not, everyone will come to the same conclusion.

Unleash the Big Shoes: Giving Your Team a Chance to Show You What's Possible

"At this point in my career and in my life, I recognize more than ever the importance of investing in the development of others."

~ Kathleen M. Mazarella, CEO, Graybar Electric

Be open-minded about who your leaders are.

Who is the untapped talent in your organization? You may have leaders amid the masses but be completely unaware of it because you haven't given them the chance to shine. You don't need to create the most exciting environment to do this; you simply need to create leadership opportunities and see who takes the first bite at the apples you set out.

Olympic athlete Stacy Dragila was the first woman to ever pole vault in the Olympics for the United States—because her coach took a shot on the chance that she "might" be some untapped potential.

Stacy was attending Idaho State University when she began her career as a heptathlete. The sport of pole vaulting was just becoming available to women athletes, and her coach encouraged her to try it.

Although she took to the sport, she was not exactly an Olympian when she first started, and "clumsy" is the word she used to describe her early career to the *San Francisco Chronicle*. But her coach saw something in her that went beyond her athletic talent—that spark that every coach, every teacher, every leader hopes to see in the people they are motivating and inspiring.

Stacy went on to become the first dominant female pole-vaulter in history, setting a number of world records in the process. She earned world titles in 1997, 1999, and 2001, but the high point of her career was the gold medal she took home from Sydney, Australia, for the 2000 Olympic Team. Today, Stacy is a coach at Rocky Mountain High, doing the exact same thing her own coach did: scouting out the untapped leaders and nurturing any spark she can find.

1. **Find out what your people need to be successful, and create a learning organization.**

   ❖ Learning fosters pride and a sense of connection with the company.

   ❖ It also improves employee engagement and significantly reduces turnover. Companies we surveyed show vast needs in the area of effective communication, leadership development, time management, and keeping staff members accountable.

2. **Allow your people to develop the skills they need to perform optimally, and challenge them to build skill sets that are beyond their current positions.**

   ❖ Allowing employees to shadow jobs in other divisions or orienting them to the entire company helps them to see the big picture and understand the vast potential of the company.

   ❖ As staff members rise to the top, look to the horizon, and plan for succession.

   ❖ Groom your ideal replacement as you continue to grow and advance yourself as well.

3. **Create a mentoring culture where leaders support one another.**

   ❖ New leaders who become managers often try to keep doing the activities that made them successful.

   ❖ The skills needed for new managers include planning, filling jobs, assigning work, motivating, coaching, and measuring the success of others.

❖ Reallocate their time from performing work to helping others perform effectively and delegating. Reallocating this time is difficult for many new leaders, as they have yet to learn the value of "management work" compared to the work that made them successful.

❖ Once they learn how to help others to be successful by managing their time, assignments, and resources, they create a successful culture of motivated performers.

4. Bring coaching competencies in-house.

❖ Coaching represents the most significant trend in leadership development within the last 25 years. You might wonder if coaching is any more effective than giving advice or direction, but coaching has been proven to decrease turnover by increasing loyalty and employee engagement.

❖ Managers who report to senior managers who are skilled in coaching outperform their peers by 27 percent.

❖ Employees who work for leaders who have been trained in coaching say they feel more valued and satisfied with their jobs, and, in turn, put greater effort into their work.

5. Know you have a potential to tap as well, so don't forget to continue your own personal growth and development.

❖ Rub elbows with other Renegade Leaders, join in our virtual community.

❖ Share your visions with like-minded executives who are equally committed to success.

❖ Stay informed and get the resources you need to stay relevant and to make informed decisions.

6. **Allow others to "fail forward."**

    ❖ Taking risks is part of unleashing potential. Sometimes the wrong choice is made, but without risk companies cannot grow. Guide your people to take calculated risks.

    ❖ Again, if you are clear as a leader, they will make decisions based on the shared values and goals of the organization.

    ❖ When an error is made, acknowledge the person's willingness to move forward.

Engage in Transparent Communication

"Focus on constant iteration of your product or service. Never hold too closely to your idea but be open to change an innovation."

~ Jean Chong, Co-Founder and CEO, Starbates

We've talked and talked and talked (I am a woman!) about communication. Your people want to hear from you, so be clear with them about who you are, what your story is, where you are taking them, and keep them updated. When you share your vision, you allow others to add to it. Empower your vision by letting those closest to the customer, to the production floor, to your customers, or in your industry engage in the conversation.

1. **Assess your current means of communication.**

    ❖ Is it effective?

    ❖ Does it provide timely information?

    ❖ Are all departments aware of each other's goals, and are the overall goals of your organization discussed frequently?

    ❖ What is missing?

2. **Ask your teams to design an effective system for transparent communication.**

   ❖ What do they want to hear about?

   ❖ What are the most important topics?

   ❖ How can the system give voice to employees?

   ❖ How will the executive team share information?

3. **Decide on a platform that is secure and easy for all personnel to use.**

   ❖ Look into both in-house and web-based platforms.

4. **Determine what topics of communication you can maintain.**

   ❖ Will there be a human resources area for benefits?

   ❖ A CEO newsletter?

   ❖ An operations portal?

   ❖ What about "In the News," "What we are doing in the community," or a "Shout Out" area for recognizing achievements?

5. **Once you have the basic structure set up, consider using an assessment service to provide polls to quickly collect data from your employees.**

6. **Give a face to your communications through videos, which are fast, effective, and preferred by all types of learners.**

7. **Decide on the frequency of updates from executives.**

   ❖ Once a number is determined, keep your promise, posting as often as you have decided. Old blog posts quickly become stale.

8. **Develop an implementation rollout plan.**

   ❖ One plan that has been used successfully is to begin with the executive team allowing key pages to be populated, followed by managers, and, finally, all employees.

9. **Consider allowing employees to have their own pages where they can post information, allowing them to get to know one another better.**

   ❖ What else can be added that will build a family-like atmosphere, even if your locations are continents apart?

10. **Develop a "how-to" guide to educate users on how to post, your posting protocol, on how the site will be monitored, and on what types of posts go where.**

11. **Launch the site by scheduling site enrollment days.**

   ❖ Local managers can inspire enrollments by making access something valuable and desired.

12. **Start to connect, engage, and weave unity throughout your organization, truly sharing the spirit of navigation toward your goals with authenticity and transparency.**

Notice and Recognize Achievements

> *"Everyone has an invisible sign hanging from their necks saying, 'Make me feel important.' Never forget this message when working with people."*
>
> ~ Mary Kay Ash, Founder Mary Kay Cosmetics

1. **Encourage employees to recognize one another.**

   ❖ Acknowledge "above and beyond" behavior.

❖ Use storytelling to showcase top performances by relating to everyone what the employee did, what results occurred, and why this ties into the shared values and vision of the organization. (We showcase Renegade Leaders in our "Who's been spotted" segment of our newsletter. Perhaps we will showcase you!)

2. **Create performance-based rewards.**

❖ Determine what rewards matter most to your employees, and establish a standard for recognizing high performance with financial benefits, upgraded title, schedule flexibility, and other rewards.

3. **Practice day-to-day recognition, and train your management teams to do the same.**

❖ Know what praise and appreciation works for the person you are acknowledging, and customize your efforts.

❖ Write a note to the individual or his/her family, indicating his/her value to the company.

❖ Take a staff member out to lunch; one-on-one time is highly valued if you can spare it.

❖ Use your company newsletter or communication portal to give credit where it is due. Share recognition with your customers on company wins as well as client successes (with their permission, of course).

4. **Be creative; rewards don't have to cause a strain on your finances.**

❖ Build a goal thermometer to help teams achieve a goal. Keep it visual, and make it fun.

❖ Use small gifts to show your appreciation. *www.baudville.com* has tons of offerings from thumbs-up tokens to other items.

❖ Use everyday items to show value: a stick of gum to say someone is "sticking with the project"; glue for "holding the team together"; and so on. Don't laugh! These little tokens, which seem small, can have big value. What can you use?

5. **Schedule appreciation for others into your day, making it part of your routine.**

❖ Showing gratitude actually reduces your blood pressure, causes a great release of serotonin for both you and the recipient, and creates a feel-good culture.

Culture: Create a Culture of Collaboration Toward a Vision

> *"Walt Disney told his crew to 'build the castle first' when constructing Disney World, knowing that vision would continue to serve as motivation throughout the project. Oftentimes when people fail to achieve what they want in life, it's because their vision isn't strong enough."*
>
> ~ Gail Blanke, President and CEO, Lifedesigns

The word "collaboration" is used frequently today in organization and business recommendations. Why is this important? It produces results. It contributes to that sense of family that is going to keep a team loyal and successful. But those are just two reasons. If you're going to climb the ladder of influence, fostering collaboration will get you higher, faster. It's not just about the culture that your work environment creates; it's about that spark that is in the air. That sense that the people on the team can go to anyone, anytime, for anything, without having to worry about...anything.

And you created it. Like that quiet collaborative tone that underlies every gathering of family or friends, it's the hum of the girls' night out where everybody is simply in it together no matter what. So how do you get your team collaborating more?

1. **Make your goal a destination, and share it vividly.**

   ❖ Describe it using all of your senses, and keep it alive with a visual, compelling image.

2. **Appeal to others to join you on the journey, allowing them to add their paint colors to the canvas.**

   ❖ Talk about why this work, project, or destination matters, and how it ties into the core values and commitments of the organization.

   ❖ Win over anyone who is reluctant by making the vision relevant to them and giving it personal meaning.

3. **Track the mile markers along the way, and wave the flag to encourage movement.**

   ❖ Stay agile enough to change direction or take a more scenic route when necessary.

4. **Create opportunities to use the collective intelligence.**

   ❖ Ask others to take on tasks, to drive the project home, or to complete its road map.

   ❖ Develop task groups or focus groups, and make it part of your routine to talk about and create the future.

5. **Spend some time at the destination.**

   ❖ Too often, Renegade Leaders are so happy when a project or action is complete that another is quickly assigned before there is time to relish the accomplishment.

   ❖ Take time to look at what you and your teams created, and take it in before the sandcastle disappears.

Encouraging Respect and Diversity
in your Organization

*"If we are to achieve a richer culture, rich in contrasting values,
we must recognize the whole gamut of human potentialities,
and so weave a less arbitrary social fabric, one in which each
diverse gift will find a fitting place."*

~ Margaret Mead

Today most organizations realize the value of diversity and even have programs to promote diversity awareness; however, many don't build in diversity awareness to enable employees to understand and benefit from others' cultures. One manager of Asian descent said, "When I am quiet, I am very engaged," yet her team thought of her as quiet and unresponsive. Diversity provides richness to organizations that can't be denied.

1. **Gain awareness of and accept your own cultural programming, which impacts your thinking and behaviors, and consider this programming when engaging with others.**

   ❖ Read about diversity, and self-assess the thoughts and behaviors you might have about others.

   ❖ Look at your organization and assess how diversity is respected.

   ❖ Develop flexibility with people who are culturally different, get to know their world views, and understand how their views influence them in the workplace.

2. **Take a stand against stereotyping.**

   ❖ As I learned in my multicultural training, if you are not taking a stand, you are part of the problem.

   ❖ Have the courage to speak out against mean comments, stereotypes, bias, and demeaning or hurtful statements.

They have no place in your organization because these are the attitudes and behaviors that prevent inclusion and teamwork.

3. **Get to know the landscape of your organization.**

   ❖ What is your cultural makeup?

   ❖ Do you have a road map for its navigation? Learn more about the culture that exists within your organization. For example, read *Coaching Across Cultures* by Phillip Rosinski, which groups cultural orientations into categories that are of importance to leaders.

   ❖ If you really want to unleash the fullest potential in your people, as well as within your organization, it's key to understand the cultural differences of your employees. Besides the obvious, these differences can relate to a sense of power and responsibility, time management approaches, definition of identity and purpose, boundary specifications, modes of thinking, or communication patterns.

4. **Make inclusion part of your organizational plan.**

   ❖ What are you currently doing to encourage respect for others' ideas?

   ❖ Are you inviting ideas from everyone?

   ❖ What professional development might you or your teams need in order to understand diversity?

5. **Encourage talent diversity in your organization.**

   ❖ Most of the time, when people think of respect and diversity, there is a significant emphasis on race, sex, and skin color. Few people consider talent diversity in an organization.

❖ Urge people to respect one another's diverse talents. Understand the value of each individual including the generational preferences.

❖ If possible, have some of your more influential team members spend time observing other departments or working alongside people who perform tasks different from theirs. After all, nothing cultivates mutual respect and understanding like walking in another person's shoes. You'll find that the more you encourage people to respect diversity of talent, the more encouraged they'll be to respect diversity of all kinds.

6. **Continue to look for, recognize, and value diversity.** It makes your journey far more scenic, and it enriches your experience and the experience of others.

Focus on What You Can Influence

You can't do it all at once. Focus on what you can influence. It is easy to fall into the trap of focusing on what isn't working or on the responsibilities that line today's in-box. A leader of an organization focuses on the big picture and backs a cultural engagement plan that will support the organization and its future, one that inspires its current employees and attracts top talent.

Some of the CEOs I interviewed worried that their people didn't seem to appreciate all that they did for them. Know that at any time, you can't keep everybody happy.

Richard Hackman blogged about teamwork and harmony for the *Harvard Business Review* and said that the perception that harmony is necessary is a misconception. He showed research showing that when conflict is well managed and focused, it can inspire creativity.

When many different people are disagreeing about a project, the leaders in those groups will rise to the challenge of collaborating and finding creative solutions to different problems.

Oprah Winfrey has been quoted as saying, "Lots of people want to ride with you in the limo, but what you want is someone who will take the bus with you when the limo breaks down."

Your team is going to have struggle and conflict on occasion, and you will exhaust yourself trying to smooth it over every single time. Instead, sit back and let them face those challenges together; let them figure out how to cooperate in a way that will eventually lead to a successful outcome.

Set clear expectations. This includes what is and what is not acceptable. Dr. Phil calls it "teaching people how to treat you." Be clear about your expectations without apology.

Women have a bigger problem with this than men; but at the Sunday dinner table, we don't have a problem nipping something in the bud and clearly stating, "I want you to stop doing that immediately." We need to follow through at work with this same mentality. This is precisely what CEO of Xerox, Ursula Burns, said at the annual *Fortune Magazine* Most Powerful Women Summit. She said once she got over the hurdle of saying "I want you to do this" instead of "Would you mind or could you please do this," she found the wheels of collaboration started to roll.

Focus on your talents of bringing people together. Rather than spend hours scouring the journals on the best methods to create bottom-line results, think about what you do best with other people in your life, and expand on that in the workplace.

Marissa Mayer knew she was going to get hit with criticism when she chose to terminate the telecommuting option at Yahoo, but she had a plan—something that is now known as the "PB&J meeting." Everyone at Yahoo meets once a week for a Friday Town Hall meeting to discuss how to deal with issues related to Process, Bureaucracy, and

Jams, or PB&J. It was catchy, and gave everyone that warm, fuzzy, right-at-home feeling that she wanted.

The night after her first PB&J meeting, she blasted an e-mail to all 12,000 Yahoo employees expressing her commitment to making Yahoo "the absolute best place to work." What self-respecting employee would *not* want to make a commitment to collaboration in that kind of culture?

Collaboration isn't rocket science. It's about using what you are already good at to inspire the people around you. It's not something you need to think about. In fact, the more you think about it, the more likely you are to stray from the path. Sometimes it is as simple as PB&J.

HOW TO MAKE SURE YOUR BEST SHOES LAST

Once you've climbed the ladder to the point where you're leading an organization, you want to make sure that organization is around for the long haul. So what can you do to make sure your shoes are around even longer than you are?

In an effort to find out, Shell Corporation funded the Long-Lived Company Study. This study determined the key components of longevity after assessing companies that were 200 or more years old. The study revealed that these companies saw themselves as a community first and a profit center second. Their cultures had a sense of identity and shared values. They focused on culture—a way of "being" that promoted success—and their culture was reflected in their processes and systems, as well as how they interacted with employees, customers, stakeholders, and their community at large. There was a tolerance and openness, and everyone shared in fiscal awareness and social consciousness.

Culture is defined as a shared belief system of values and processes within an organization. It has been described simply as "the way we do things." It is a powerful component to any organization and has both explicit and implicit characteristics.

Corporate culture is a philosophy to guide organizational strategy, workforce behavior, and management attitudes. Leadership is considered the key element for defining and driving workplace culture. Through your leadership style, you can shape and develop your company's culture in the same way you develop sales, operations, or marketing.

It all starts with you.

What can you do to ensure your organization's sustainability? Renegade Leadership is the beginning. Creating a culture that resonates with the 21st-century workforce ensures your ability to lead others with certainty. This type of leadership requires heavy work: laying down the foundations of trust, building the pillars of shared values, allowing collaboration and joint leadership, and making room for transparent communication and innovation.

Lay the tracks for innovation. Create a company focused on the future. Give opportunities for employees to visualize, getting excited about what is possible.

Use your feminine swagger. The "people-centered" style of management is what leads to greater success. This approach means relinquishing control to others and trusting that employees will not abuse that responsibility.

However, you can see that the payoffs are well worth it when your people are:

- Able to perform at the peak of their potential.

- Connected to the company and its vision.

- Motivated to go above and beyond perfunctory performance.

- Responsible concerning their role in the company.

- Passionate about the success of the company and the actions they can take to ensure that success.

The effects of people-centered leadership on your bottom line are eye-opening. Performance isn't the only thing that soars; profits also soar. With increased engagement, teams function better, tasks are performed with ease, little time is wasted, and there is greater commitment to improving the bottom line in all areas.

The executives and business owners who become exemplary Renegade Leaders all gain an increase in both performance and profits. *CFO* magazine reports that Best Buy experiences a $100,000 increase in net operating income for every tenth of a point increase in employee engagement. What would happen if you simply moved your employees' level of engagement by just a fraction?

What does it take for you to step fully into your power? When facing industry changes, it is all you can do to stand strong and inspire your people to do the same.

Meet Lisa Guertin,
President and General Manager, Anthem Blue Cross
and Blue Shield

Lisa greeted me with an enthusiastic smile. Her warmth and radiant energy were very welcoming, and she was ready to share her advice for the readers of *Running in High Heels*.

Lisa took her current position in 2011 after having been with the company for 23 years. She had previously served as New Hampshire's State Plan President from 2004 to 2008 and, as president and general manager, is now involved in corporate strategy, planning, and execution, and will serve as the primary contact for state regulators and elected officials.

For the past three years, Lisa served as senior vice president of commercial marketing for Anthem's parent company. In that role, she was responsible for product management, product development, and marketing for the local group, national accounts, and specialty and UniCare customers, representing more than 80 percent of the company's membership. Lisa has been with the company since 1990 and previously held a number of leadership positions within the organization. Overall, she has more than 25 years of diverse experience in the health insurance industry, including sales, marketing, operations, and communications.

Lisa is an example of a leader who exemplifies the L.E.A.D Forward Formula™. She leveraged her career, focuses on engaging her people, activates a culture that can flex to change and focuses on not only the brand of her company but establishing her personal brand.

"I was promoted and advanced my career because I was recognized for my contributions. My advice to other women is to do your work well; take on challenging tasks."

"Everyone has a brand, whether you believe you do or not. If you don't manage your brand, it will take on its own form" and perhaps not be what you wanted. Lisa credits her success to trusting her team and in building a culture of high performance. *"Culture matters; people need to work together; there are no turf wars here. We have fun together but work hard to serve our customers and to work as a team together."*

We discussed the importance of leaders having great people around them, and Lisa noted the importance of *"trusting your team of people, allowing them to be influential in decisions and to be creative in their 'area of brilliance' to build cohesion and collaboration."*

"Emotional Intelligence in important—knowing how to engage with and flux with other people." We also discussed the value of what I refer to as "guiding principles" and she refers to as *"norms." "People need to know what is expected of them and what behaviors and attitudes are expected. Leaders set the tone by modeling this behavior."*

Lisa's style of leadership resonates with what we believe to be the top leadership values. She is a model of its core values, demonstrating how to act as a leader, enabling others to act, encouraging the heart, challenging processes, and inspiring a shared vision. Her town hall meetings offer the opportunity for people to be seen, heard, and noticed within the organization.

Lisa values coaching and mentoring—*"we need more truth tellers"*—to provide feedback, guide behaviors, and demonstrate leadership. With all of the changes in healthcare, is it nice to know that Lisa is at the helm, making decisions that sustain her business, serve her employees, and offer the best of care and services to her clients.

STEPPING FORWARD: IN SUMMARY, IN ACTIVATE YOU LEARNED:

1. How to create a culture steeped in the richness of collaboration and creativity, positioning it and you for sustainable success.

2. The I.N.F.L.U.E.N.C.E. Framework™ and how to activate positive shifts in culture change.

3. The questions to continue to ask yourself as you scan the horizon of your culture frequently.

4. How top CEOs manage their culture while keeping balance in their own life.

Get your "Activate" gifts at:

http://www.therenegadeleader.com/BookResources

This was the letter "A" for Activate in the
L.E.A.D. Forward Formula™.

Next is "**D**" for Distinguish.

The L.E.A.D. Formula™ has stepped us from Leveraging your
leadership, Engaging with others, and Activating a culture of positivity
and possibility. Now, let's look at Distinguishing yourself and your
organization.

It's easy to blend in, more fun to stand out.

7 $\mathcal{D}$ISTINGUISH: HOW TO DISTINGUISH YOURSELF AND YOUR ORGANIZATION

Many leaders focus on how to leverage their leadership, engage their people, and activate a high-performance, aligned culture. Few spend as much time thinking about distinguishing themselves and their brand

The next letter in the L.E.A.D. Forward Framework™ is "D" for Distinguish. The good news is that you get to "define" your brand as well as that of your organization.

Many of my clients didn't start out planning to have a brand platform for themselves, but that is what happened when we worked together. By developing a clear message and brand, one client was pursued and recently interviewed by the *New York Times* and *Wall Street Journal,* recognized as a thought leader. Others are sought after as top leaders and asked to share their wisdom as keynote speakers; one made the cover of *Smart CEO* magazine. Another was asked to speak in Washington, DC about the mission of her business; two produced bestselling books; I just submitted comments for another who is publishing a manifesto about the success of their culture, which utilized executive coaching and leadership development to become a recognized Best Business of the Year; and another is launching her brand and own product line, which will lead to a passive revenue stream long after she exits her CEO chair.

When you lead from a place of innovation, impact, and influence your brand starts to form. A brand isn't developed; it is what others think of you. Your company has a brand; do you?

You recognize distinction. For some organizations distinction is its own allure: Jaguar's brand offers exclusivity and Apple is for a culture of people who wanted something different. For others it is a way of being both as an individual and as a company, such as Virgin and Richard Branson.

As Lisa Guertin mentioned in the previous chapter, you are a brand. Your company is a brand. In today's competitive market you and your company need to be seen above the radar.

We've all seen it. You are sitting in a restaurant enjoying your dinner and the company you keep.

And in she walks.

You can almost sense her coming as you start to notice the heads of others turning. She's well-dressed, but something else about her draws your attention. She seems very confident, and she must be, according to her shoes. You notice how the tan uppers of her spectator pumps contrast against the jet black heels and how, as she walks by, a flash of a red sole comes as a surprise.

You wonder how she could possibly wear such high heels and still walk with grace. You might even yearn to have your own pair in your closet. Or at least feel comfortable enough to wear them if you wanted to.

The truth is you can turn heads with or without the sky-high Louboutins. It doesn't matter if you are a stiletto women, prefer black pumps, are fond of flats, or are a dyed-in-the-wool Birkenstock girl; every leader needs a platform, a consistency in how you show up each and every day. You consider it when you open your closet in the morning; why not consider your platform the wardrobe you show to others?

DEVELOP AND TELL YOUR STORY

Everyone loves a story. Learn how to tie your own laces together.

In his famous Stanford University commencement speech, Steve Jobs talked about connecting the dots of his life. That is the first step in developing your platform.

> *"You can't connect the dots looking forward; you can only connect them looking backward. So you have to trust that the dots will somehow connect in your future. You have to trust in something—your gut, destiny, life, karma, whatever. Because believing that the dots will connect down the road will give you the confidence to follow your heart, even when it leads you off the well-worn path; and that will make all the difference."*
>
> *~ Steve Jobs*

It made me think of the "dots" in my own life. If I didn't know how to create sales, I wouldn't know how to get business results for my clients. If I hadn't studied psychology, I might not understand what motivates people or how to shift the thoughts, beliefs, and behaviors needed for high performance and increased employee engagement. If large sales didn't force me into national global account management for my clients, I wouldn't have had to learn how to lead more effectively, and if life didn't have its own challenges along the way, my inner Renegade Leader might not have been unleashed.

When I started coaching leaders, my goal was to help them build teams that were inspired and fueled more by their energy than their morning cup of coffee.

I had seen that lack of inspiration before, in my own life when I didn't have what I was expecting in my family, when I wasn't given my permission slip to shine because my environment wasn't one to nourish my brilliance.

Then it dawned on me: Companies are like families, and the CEOs and executives are like the parents in those families. I connected the dots. Now I combine my career success in the world of corporate sales and my expertise as a licensed psychologist and internationally certified executive coach with my earliest life lessons to help my clients create in their family what I didn't have in my family and what is missing in most organizations: harmony, peace, collaboration, and validation.

Now it's time for you to connect your dots and to create your brand story.

Start in your own shoes. What traits were present in your early years that would become the fiber of your leather later on? Look at the decisions you made along the way. Are there any common threads, like the criteria you used to make decisions? What values are you starting to see that rise to the top again and again? What bold moves did you make even if their success was not guaranteed? Even if you had bumps in the road or dipped around potholes on the way, what did you take away from those experiences? What has become ingrained—and in looking it over, does it still serve you?

Look over the horizon of your work experience. What have you learned during your journey that helps you today? What experiences have you had that make you unique? Can you identify how those experiences might be related to your work, career, or leadership choices?

What are you passionate about? What makes you feel your best? What can you *not* not do, it comes so naturally?

In your dots lies a story that will set you apart from all others. It is this story that will set the design for your personal brand, your signature presence, your personal fingerprint. Building the story with my clients is fun as we go on an amazing journey back in time to see how their life weaved their beautiful fabric together.

The most powerful leaders share their story. Story Stylist Gayle Nowark states that *"if you're struggling to shower the world in your brilliance, you need to release the story hiding inside of you and learn how to use it to build profitable, meaningful relationships with your customers."* I'd add your employees and your industry to that list. CEOs also need the support of the media—and to become a "media darling," the first step is connecting the dots and building your own story so that others will want to hear it.

At this juncture your impulse might be to push back. You might feel uncomfortable with what I am suggesting, or you may want to ask, "Will people accept my story; is it good enough?" "How is my story related to who I am now; will it make sense; is it necessary?" People buy from who they know and knowing you through your story will build greater trust from your employees, from your customers, and in your industry. It just takes courage to step into your unique story.

Lisa Guertin advised you to manage your own brand or one will be developed for you. Your brand is not what was developed for you but who really are. People want to know your human side. When you stand in your story you stand in your authenticity. Take the time to know and develop your story.

CREATING A PLATFORM

Much has been written about developing a platform and it's not the shoe I am referring to. It is no longer good enough to offer a great product or service; you have to stand out, create a wave, or ride a trend. You have to have a presence in every social media portal, develop a community, be transparent as a leader, and share what you stand for so you stand together with your people.

How you are seen, heard, and noticed both as a leader and as an organization is really all up to your own design. As the leader of an organization, the platform begins with you. It's time to be seen and get noticed in a cluttered world. Think about other organizations you know. Richard Branson and his Virgin brand are known for their Renegade attitude. Tony Hsieh wrote *Delivering Happiness* to showcase the fun, zany culture of Zappos that provides the wow factor in their platform.

If I walked up and down the hallways of your company, what would your people say is your platform? What do you stand for?

In our earlier chapters, you learned to identify your leadership style, your values, and your must-have, authentic leadership traits. How are they showing up in your work? Building a platform is about understanding who you are at the foundational level and constructing it from there. It allows you to walk unapologetically and powerfully.

A brand promotes visibility; it puts you front and center. It amplifies your message above all of the noise; it enables you to be heard above the roar of the crowd. It offers connection. People connect to what they resonate with; it attracts fans, customers, and high-performing talent to your door.

When Wendy Tirollos's team at TRM Microwave told me they do the "tough jobs no one else wants, we figure it out," I saw that as their wow—their unique brand. A design, engineering, and manufacturing company that supports the defense, aerospace, and commercial industry run by a woman is also a unique brand. Its 43-year history of business and being selected by the largest of companies to serve as their provider shows that TRM has built its unique platform as the go-to company in its industry. Both she and her company have a brand that sets them apart.

CHOOSE THE SHOE STYLE
THAT SETS YOU APART

Meet Jo Ellen Nash,
CEO Naples Luxury Real Estate Group

Luxury Real Estate CEO Jo Ellen Nash knows how to set her business apart from the rest. A leader in her industry, she specializes in luxury estates, waterfront homes, and golf communities in Naples, Florida. During her 30-year career, she has served more than 2,000 families with their real estate needs and has been honored with multiple awards, including the Overall Marketing Excellence Award at the Leaders in Luxury Conference and the Luxury Conclave, awards for Best Personal Website and Best Personal Branding, recognition as a *STAR* agent in the elite Star Power Network, a Cyber Star, and one of the first agents ever to be certified as a Luxury Home Marketing Specialist.

Jo Ellen is also a business strategist who leads the luxury coaching program at CKG International. A well-known speaker and contributor to her profession, she shares her expertise with others to help them improve their businesses. And if that's not enough, Jo Ellen now also operates her own marketing company, Nash Signature Marketing, which focuses on developing branding strategies and marketing materials for select agents around North America.

Jo Ellen and I enjoyed a deep conversation about overcoming barriers to success by using the time management and leadership strategies she utilizes as part of her daily rituals.

"Learn to leverage yourself so that you have time to put the big rocks in first." Many business owners think of the "big rocks" as big business goals; however, Jo Ellen and other successful business owners know this means to put yourself, your relationships, and even your faith in first. Robert G. Allen, real estate guru and author of *No Money Down,* said the same thing to me when I had the luxury of visiting him in his home in San Diego. You can't have a successful career if you have ill health or if your relationships are broken.

Jo Ellen explained, *"I have a successful business. I believe in having outstanding systems in my business so it runs successfully."* Her systems include hiring excellent people, delegating, building a strong team, and time blocking so everything runs proficiently and with ease. *"Everything you do more than once needs a system."* We agreed that too many leaders spend their day in crisis management—"putting out fires."

Jo Ellen handles everything proactively; she provides excellent service to her clients. She manages multiple companies and services with ease by managing client expectations and building the systems needed to meet their needs. She also realizes, as a business owner and as a branding and marketing company, the importance of being unique. While other real estate organizations were quaking in fear of a falling market, Jo Ellen was moving full speed ahead, outfitting her spa-like office with a waterfall, art gallery, and Internet station. She provided luxury service to her clientele, offering a limo service to pick them up, moving trucks to get them settled into their new homes, and services and personal attention that made them feel valued and part of an exclusive club.

She also offers a coveted Naples "State of the Market Report" and "Seller Marketing Report" that alert her clients to current information on properties, reports as professional and innovative as Jo Ellen is herself. She knows not only how to run successful businesses but also when to invest in her clients in order to distinguish her business as top-of-the-line.

She sees her business as a concierge service, serving her clients like her closest friends. This includes making her clients a part of her life, hosting gatherings of 200 or more at her own home. Making personal connections with clients brings her great joy and personalizes her service. As a result, those clients refer to her again and again. She realizes the value of growth through partnership with others and has grown a vast referral-based business. She coaches other agents to adopt her philosophies and systems for success in her Nash Signature Marketing programs.

Her advice to other leaders is to "*begin with those big rocks, create structure in your businesses, time block, build systems, hire excellent people, and be dedicated to your clients. Anticipate the needs of your clients and give them an experience they may not have ever experienced before.*"

"*It's my goal to surprise and delight my clients every step of the way.*" Jo Ellen does it successfully, with ease, and in heels!

Strides for Success:

As an executive leader you might have worked with an organization to help you to define your personal brand. That is what they came up with. How you are seen in your industry, by your people, and by your stakeholders might be a different brand. What is your brand? What do you want it to be? Begin by answering the reflection questions below:

Is your brand unique, consistent, and memorable?

Is your brand trustworthy?

Does it tell your story? Show your value?

Does it offer insights into what you are passionate about?

Building your brand story is a powerful exercise. When done with leaders it promotes added confidence, spurs increased communication, gains attention from the media and industry leaders, and builds a trust foundation that serves as your float during turbulent times.

TAKING YOUR BRAND ON BOARD: WHEN ONLY A STILETTO WILL DO

Every few days, I speak with a dear friend of mine, another CEO of a fast-growing business, and she and we share our goals, our accomplishments, and our next steps. It keeps us accountable, the same way our group masterminds connect like-minded professionals together to network and achieve their goals.

One evening I was speaking with my husband, a quiet man who, at times, can grow impatient with my Renegade spirit and vast community of colleagues. I happened to mention my friend who had just called and he said, "Yes, I heard you bragging on the telephone."

Bragging on the telephone?

When did holding myself accountable, which also means reporting my wins, become bragging?

I thought about his comment for a while. I could have become angry, or I could have shouted, "Yes, we all need to brag, as that is the only way we will get validation for all that we do!"

But I didn't. Instead I took a pen and wrote this on a green three-by-three-inch sticky:

BRAG:

Bold

Responsive

Actions

for organizational Growth.

Brag. That is what I was doing: taking bold and at times stealthy moves to help my clients succeed and advance my own business.

There are times when only a stiletto will do. When you need to be seen, heard, and noticed a bit more. When you need to collect all of your accomplishments and brag just a bit.

One of those times is when women step into the boardroom.

Before I had my first son in 1988, I admired—no, coveted—that bright little yellow sticker on the back of the windshield that said "Baby on Board." While working in Boston and jet-setting back and forth to our corporate office, clients in tow and breast milk in my satchel, at times I longed to step away from it all and, as I told my husband, "be the woman in the Volvo with the Baby on Board sticker in the back."

It seemed like an easier thing to do.

But now I realize I was never meant to be the woman in the Volvo. Instead, I'm proud to be a Woman on Board—with my own seat on one of my clients' non-profit boards.

Several of the CEOs I interviewed mentioned a desire to serve on a corporate board.

So, do you have the right shoes to make the cut?

Serving on a board is a sure way to distinguish yourself and leave a lasting impact. However, right now, few seats are taken by women, and only by women who take the bold moves to claim their seat.

Catalyst's research shows women's share of corporate board seats, at 16.6 percent, hasn't grown at all since 2004. The percentage of female executive officers at Fortune 500 companies is even smaller (14.3 percent) and has remained flat for three straight years.

Why is that? And what can be done about this gender disparity? It's been proven time and time again that women bring greater success when they sit on an organization's board. Companies with female board representation routinely outperform those with no women on the board. Maybe that is why, in 2003, Norway mandated a 40-percent ratio of women on boards, or why Finland requires companies without women board members to publish the reason why in their annual reports.

What is going on in the United States? Harvard Business School Professor Boris Groysberg has incorporated a focus on gender issues into his research on drivers of individual and organizational performance. His studies include a comprehensive global survey of board members, as well as a series of case studies that approach the issue of women on boards from an individual, an organizational, and a national level. Groysberg also teaches an elective MBA course titled "How Star Women Succeed: Leading Effective Careers and Organizations."

Recently Groysberg teamed up with researcher Deborah Bell to study corporate directors around the world. Facilitated by Heidrick & Struggles and WomenCorporateDirectors (WCD), the survey compiled anonymous input from 1,067 directors in some 58 countries.

"The fact is that if you're a woman, you really have to try hard to get on boards," Groysberg says. *"There aren't too many corporate board seats that open up each year. We're not talking about millions. We're not even talking about thousands. Please. Don't tell me you can't find 100 qualified women to sit on boards in the United States of America."*

Furthermore, the personal stakes of sitting on a board are statistically higher for women than for men. For example, 90 percent of male board members are married versus 72 percent of female members, and 90 percent of the men have children versus 64 percent of the women. The divorce rate among women on boards is 10 percent versus 4 percent for men. *"So if you're a woman seeking a board seat,"* Groysberg explains, *"you have to be overqualified, and on top of that it's really hard to get in, and on top of that, once you get in there are personal costs. It's why many of the women who sit on boards are referred to as survivors."*

To achieve excellent results, companies search for qualified individuals whose skills, leadership experience, and expertise will contribute positively to the board's work, and whose personality and values interact compatibly with those of the company's other directors.

In other words, first you have to have the right shoes, and then you have to figure out if this is where you want to park them. So how do you search for a board position, if you decide you want one?

Studies have shown that women on corporate boards not only add integrity, intelligence, and business experience but also facilitate the discussion of difficult issues by forcing boards to confront the tough questions. A female contribution helps the board run in a smooth, open way.

Until now, corporations have hired traditional search firms or worked through personal relationships to identify candidates. But those sources are limited, especially when it comes to women. Women tend to be less networked than men, so boards can miss individuals who are equally as qualified as male directors—and consequently are deprived of the opportunity to benefit from the countless talents, experiences, and perspectives that female directors offer.

Former Catalyst chief Ilene Lang notes that being visible and making your accomplishments known are essential to getting the kinds of experience that can move you up into senior management, but some corporate cultures penalize women for that. Lang observes, *"It's seen as 'not ladylike' or 'too pushy.' So, to get the right opportunities, you have to be in the right culture. Find a division, or a company, where there are already some senior women, and where you'll be allowed to flourish."*

As for corporate board seats, Lang pooh-poohs the widespread notion that there just aren't enough "qualified candidates. *"The 'supply problem' is a myth,"* she says. *"But there are more qualified people than there are openings on boards, so it's very competitive. You need a champion, someone who is already 'in the club' and will vouch for you."*

To connect board-ready female executives with companies looking for directors, Catalyst launched a service called Corporate Board Resource, a clearinghouse where CEOs of Catalyst member companies—the gatekeepers of "the club"—endorse women whose experience qualifies them for board seats. *"Having the imprimatur of a CEO is tremendously powerful,"* Lang says. *"It gets you noticed in places where you otherwise wouldn't be."*

Another option is to make yourself known to board-recruiting committees like the Committee of 200, a Chicago-based non-profit organization that now numbers more than 400 high-powered women representing 100 different industries worldwide. Jan Babiak, a former Ernst & Young executive, is a Committee of 200 member who sits on three corporate boards.

"You have to treat [pursuing a board seat] like a job hunt, only with a revised resume that reflects what boards are looking for," Babiak advises. *"Reach out to your network and let people know you're looking."*

Babiak has given referrals to other women, which helped seven of them land directorships in the past year. *"Women have to support each other,"* she says. *"Other women helped me tremendously in getting my board seats, so now I'm paying it forward."* That kind of networking, which men have been doing forever, could be what finally budges the number of female directors off its current plateau.

Sitting on a board will leave a bigger heel print—and you have to ask yourself if this is a step you want take. If you do, you can see how important it is to lay the groundwork we have been talking about. To get noticed, you have to stand out in your personal brand, have your message be heard, ask for the supports you need (and get them), and position yourself and your organizational results as the strongest contender for the most sought-after seat: a seat on the board.

Is it time for you to get on board?

Success Strides:

If you are in executive leadership it is likely you already sit on a board or answer to a board. If so, take the time for board development. In the same manner you work on your culture you can sidestep the problems of most boards: not getting the work done, interpersonal conflict, disengagement, and lack of clear accountability. When we work with organizations and their board we assess the board functionality and deliver relevant solutions to optimize the board.

Look out over your board as you did your culture and ask:

Do board members perform to the best of their abilities?

Is the board aligned about strategic direction?

Does the board take responsibility for making sure that the organization is fiscally responsible?

Is the board assuring that the organization is in compliance with laws and regulations?

Does the board oversee and review the leadership team, and make sure the organization is developing new leaders and is always ready for succession?

Is the board recruiting and on-boarding other board members effectively?

Does the board know its roles and responsibilities, and does the board not overstep its boundaries (for instance by micro-managing employees or breaking the chain of command)?

Does board composition reflect the diversity of the organization's constituents?

Is the board making decisions effectively and efficiently?

KEEPING IT ALL IN BALANCE

Meet Leesa Smith,
President of Freudenberg, North America

Imagine flying across the country to Germany and being the only woman at the conference room table. That is what Leesa Smith experiences on each of her visits as president of the North American division of a multibillion-dollar global company.

Freudenberg Group and Freudenberg North America constitute a global goliath with 34,000 employees worldwide. In 2011, Leesa Smith became the organization's most senior woman when she took the helm of its North American regional holding company, which has 15 independently operated business units in industries ranging from automotive, aerospace, and medical to chemical, oil, and gas. Smith is one of three female members of the Global Executive Team (GET), making her uniquely positioned to influence both the company's finances (her specialty) and its diversity.

Leesa has been with Freudenberg for 20 years and is president of Freudenberg North America Limited Partnership, the North American holding company for Freudenberg & Co. in Germany, a family-owned company more than 160 years old. She oversees the finance, treasury, insurance, and pension functions in North America. *"We set standards and oversee key corporate initiatives,"* Leesa says of the work performed by her and her staff.

A petite yet powerful woman, Leesa welcomed me into her office with a smile. After chatting about shoes for a moment and the fun in the *Running in High Heels* title, Leesa got right down to business. Leadership and diversity are close to her heart. Leesa takes the time to mentor others; she joined me as the keynote to serve as a panelist for the University of New Hampshire's women's leadership program. We share the same values, encouraging women to expand their roles in leadership and have influence in their organizations.

She already finds time to serve on the board of directors of the Red Cross, Leadership New Hampshire, and as chair of the Red Cross "Go Red" Detroit campaign.

Leesa plans to leave a big heel print by serving on a corporate board and also bringing a leadership initiative into the company that supports other women leaders who want to have successful careers. *"Never stop growing,"* she advises.

When asked how she manages her lifestyle as a spouse and a mother, Leesa said she allocates her time, responds quickly, and gets the support that she needs in order to attend her children's events and also find some time for herself. The system must be working. Leesa hardly seemed worn for her travels, spending part of the month in two areas of the States and visiting Germany as needed. Instead, she seemed grounded, ready to make an impact, and determined to leave a legacy of heel prints for other followers.

Her advice to other women is: *"Balance is an individual concept; you have to weigh your decisions."* One decision Leesa honors is her family, making sure she attends her children's high school games. *"It's okay for you to have a personal side."* Leesa also understand how to keep her company relevant by taking the necessary risks even when the outcome isn't as predictable.

The key lesson Leesa learned along the way was that it was necessary for her to develop and manage her own brand. She advises women to *"network more and to develop a support system"*, something she initially put on the back burner.

Lisa's Advice: *"At the end of the day, you need to be your authentic self. I can swim in a shark tank and not have to change my personality,"* she says with a smile. *"It's okay to have a successful career and to be authentic."*

HOW TORY BURCH TURNED HEADS—IN FLATS

Being distinct means gaining attention for your organization and confidence in you as a leader.

There are few women who would turn down an opportunity to turn the heads of every person in the room. But while some of your female counterparts may be reading *Vogue* and *Harper's Bazaar* in order to find the perfect heel to accomplish that goal, you might be reading *Forbes* and *The New York Times* for tidbits and kernels that will get you closer to your organizational goals every day.

Like the woman who wants others to envy her Christian Louboutins, you secretly yearn to be envied when you enter the room as well.

But for different reasons.

You want people to turn their heads when you walk into the room because it's your name that everyone is reading in *Forbes*. So how do you get them *all* to turn their heads when *you* walk into a male-dominated C-suite or boardroom?

Here's how Tory Burch did it. In flats.

Tory Burch, owner and CEO of what is now a fashion empire, stated at the *Forbes* Power Redefined Women's Summit in New York that it's about forgetting that you're a woman at all. You might think it's strange for someone who makes pretty shoes for a living to "forget that she's a woman," but, according to Tory, that's not what it's about.

Former Google Empress Marissa Mayer told CNN the same thing: *"I'm not a woman at Google. I'm a geek."* Mayer's biggest piece of advice to anyone who wants to follow in similar footsteps is to remember that, at all times, passion trumps gender. She was never recognized for being a woman that was good at science—just as *someone* who was *exceptional* at science. She believes that's because her passion neutralized everything else, like her gender.

Tory Burch told the attendees of the *Forbes* Power Summit the same story, replacing computer code with color wheels. When she started her little closet business, everyone she knew, and everyone in the industry she was pitching to, thought hers was just a little "vanity project." She knew how important it would be to remember that her passion trumped all else. And, as she told *Forbes Woman* publisher Moira Forbes in a 2004 interview, her mama's advice helped, too: *"Thicken your skin."*

And thicken her skin she did. To honor her mother's advice, she created a ballet flat for just $195 and named it after her. This shoe, the Burch Reva, would become Tory's biggest hit, but not until a talk show host by the name of Oprah Winfrey featured it on her final "Favorite Things" episode.

What Tory didn't know was that her star was born the moment that episode hit the airwaves. She told the attendees of the *Forbes* Power Redefined Women's Summit, which included the likes of Secretary of Homeland Security Janet Napolitano and supermodel Christy Turlington, that she thought the whole thing was a joke. When she woke up the next morning, there were 8 million new hits on her website. Everything else after that "was a blur," and she certainly didn't take the time to wonder whether or not being a woman made a difference in her business.

Even if she wanted to, she didn't have the time. She was too busy joining the ranks of the elite, 2013 *Forbes* World's Billionaires. But Tory's circle is even more elite than that circle of *Forbes*-honored men and women. She is one of only three women on that list who made her own fortune. The other two are Meg Whitman and the lady who ran a talk show and gave away some pretty shoes one day.

Tory Burch is now 46 years old and the second-youngest self-made billionaire in America. Since her pretty flats showed up on Oprah's list of Favorite Things, her annual income is estimated at $800 million.

Building the platform you need to turn heads when you enter the room can be done. As Marissa Mayer and Tory Burch show us, it's not about being the one who has the highest heel. Sometimes the only way to truly stand a head above everybody else in the male-dominated C-suite is to strap on the flats, thicken up the skin, and follow the passion that got you there in the first place.

Those bold moves make an effective leader.

Current studies show that women leaders have moved the needle in risk taking; the difference between men and women is that we take more calculated risks. We take in the big picture and weigh the total impact of taking the risk: the impact on the business, the employees, the industry, and even our own lives.

The most successful women I know take steps in quantum leaps. A friend of mine says that life is like being on a trapeze: You have to let go before swinging to connect again to what is on the other side. It's the hanging in the middle that can be the scariest part.

Part of standing out in your brand is making your dreams public proclamations. My husband laughed when I started to write the first sentences of *The Renegade Leader: 9 Success Strategies Driven Leaders Use to Ignite People, Performance and Profits*. On my side of our bathroom mirror, I posted a sticky note that said "Best-Selling Author."

He laughed—and then he didn't when, within weeks of its publication, it hit #1 on the Amazon Best Seller List in Business & Motivation and #2 in Self-Improvement.

Late one night, when I saw that the Academy of Television Arts & Sciences was planning to provide books from four national authors in the Emmy Awards goody bags, I didn't hesitate to put my book on the runway for consideration. My book was selected, and I have pictures of it being embraced by the stars of *Homeland, Glee, Dexter,* and many other critically honored television series.

Taking risks and being seen above the clutter is part of what I teach my clients to do. Big dreams don't happen in baby steps, it takes a quantum leap.

SOMETIMES THE POWER OF YOUR BRAND IS IN SHOWING UP WHERE NO ONE ELSE HAS BEEN

Meet Kathy Eberwein,
President, Managing Director, Global Edge Consultants

In a world where 85 percent of businesses fold during their first five years, and more diminish in the years that follow, most leaders would like to know how to follow Kathy Eberwein's path. After five years, her company is on track for $65 million, and she plans to take it all the way to $500 million.

Trained as an engineer, Kathy stumbled into technical recruiting and immediately discovered a passion for it. She was instrumental in the development of U.S. operations for two global oil and gas staffing firms, and as she continued to develop relationships in the industry, began to visualize having a company of her own. So she laid the groundwork for a strong female-owned company that would flourish around the world. She started The Global Edge Consultants in May 2008. Based in Spring, Texas, The Global Edge Consultants is one of the fastest-growing oil and gas recruitment firms in North America, employing more than 26 recruitment staff and with offices in Maryland, Arizona, Singapore, Canada, Mozambique, Indonesia, South Africa, Australia, and the UK.

Kathy is proud to have one of the first woman-owned staffing firms committed to going global in support of the oil and gas industry. She and her team have far surpassed their initial goals since opening the doors in 2008. When asked what lies ahead, Kathy says, *"We expect to be on every continent in the next three years."* With a proven track record and a big vision, the best may be yet to come for The Global Edge.

I asked Kathy where her ambition started. *"I learned the value of hard work at an early age by watching other business owners and by being exposed to new things"*. Sister to Jo Ellen Nash, her world was expanded every summer when her parents, both teachers, took them on the road, camping, visiting new locations, and exposing them to new learning.

As a busy single mother of four children, Kathy knows the power of focus, faith, goal-setting, and determination leads to success. *"It's essential to be focused on your vision; you need to know it through and through."* Having little time for the drama of leadership, she focuses on what she considers *"the six most important things to do each and every day,"* and as a result is not reactive but proactive, focused, and able to achieve more through effective strategy.

Part of Kathy's vision is in *"creating and maintaining a great place to work"* so her company focuses on its culture, providing excellence in service in all that they do and upholding strong ethics and integrity as a team. As a result, Global Edge has become a sought-after employer with a reputation for collaboration, creativity, and dedicated employee engagement.

Kathy believes that successful companies should use their influence to give back in the world as well. Her company has selected an initiative in every country location they are in, funding programs to reduce disease in Africa, eliminate sex trafficking in Asia, support breast cancer research, and more. Kathy also mentors young women in their 20s. *"Taking care of your people not only feels good, it makes for a successful company."*

While the company upholds its standards of excellence, it also holds fun as a key value. Kathy also offers benefits such as paternity leave and allows her staff to collaborate on decisions. *"People support what they are part of."*

As the only female business owner in her industry, Kathy's advice to other heel-wearers is: *"Do everything real well; it will come back to you. Don't worry about doing something you don't like in your career, instead do everything well and learn from what you do."*

Her most important message? *"You need to set big goals—goals that make you nervous in your stomach, something really big and scary—and then do it. Say you are going to do it and publicly proclaim it."*

Kathy intends to continue to expand the business in multiple countries. As Global Edge Consultants celebrates its fifth successful year with growth at 400 percent, she says with a laugh, *"We are adding a plaque that says 'The World is Yours'."* I'm sure for Kathy it will be—and we are all better off because she is in it.

There you have it: the L.E.A.D. Forward Formula™. In brief, this is an overview of the L.E.A.D. Forward Formula™ to:

Leverage: How to Lead with a Powerful Authentic Presence

Engage: How to Motivate and Move People to Passion, Positivity, and Possibility

Activate: How to Ignite a Culture of Collaboration and Innovation

Distinguish: How to Distinguish Yourself and Your Organization

STEPPING FORWARD: IN SUMMARY, IN DISTINGUISH YOU LEARNED:

1. How to build upon your brand through your authentic story.

2. Leading ways to leverage your board positioning.

3. What top women CEO's are doing to distinguish themselves and their organizations.

4. How to focus on your "six most important things" so you can be proactive, focused and have more time for yourself and your loved ones.

Get your "Distinguish" gifts at:

http://www.therenegadeleader.com/BookResources

8 SELF-CARE: PUTTING EXHAUSTION AWAY AS A STATUS SYMBOL

Your Pradas won't help if you are too tired to wear them.

You run a lesser risk of breaking a heel if you get the support you need. Leaders need help but don't ask for it, especially women. Leadership can take the best out of you, if you let it.

Do you ever say yes to something you should have said no to? Many of my clients tell me that they work well into the wee hours just to get everything done.

I understand doing the work because you love what you are doing, but I also know that to keep it in balance, we can't do it all alone.

When you think about it, as leaders, we are always "on." Cell phones, Tweets, Facebook, and LinkedIn communications don't make it easy to step away. I was on my way to the ladies' room when the *Miami Herald* called me asking for an opinion on Sheryl Sandberg's book, *Lean In,* and my take on working moms and leadership. Luckily, I wasn't in the stall just yet but if I had been, I'm proud to say my kegels are up to date.

When it comes to working after hours, I know we women aren't alone. My male clients tell me that they do their work on vacation; CEOs check on the office during early-morning hours while the family sleeps. Which is nice—but they're probably not also packing the luggage, planning the meals, and making sure the bathing suits are washed.

Meet Lisa Allen,
Chief Administrative Officer, GNHR

As women we need to own our choices. Lisa, a CAO, chose to talk about choices in her interview. A driven visionary she loves her work and is passionate about the organization's success as well as her own. As we sat together Lisa talked about the choices women make and why it is important to honor the choices you made without regret.

"Women can experience power leaks, and one way to get off center is to agonize over the choices we make." Worrying that *"I left my poor baby sitting in the hall waiting for me"* or *"I missed my son's game"* is useless when, at those moments, there was an important choice to make and the choice was made for a good reason. *"Driving out of the parking lot agonizing over a decision isn't going to do you, your family, or your organization any good."*

Make your choices with discretion. Lisa describes with a laugh how on her most recent vacation, she packed all four suitcases—two for her and her husband and two for her children—while they sat in the car waiting for her to come out so they could go. *"I took care of it all,"* she says with a sigh. She weighs the choices she makes over our afternoon lunch, surrounded by the chatter of excited voices on a sunny day. *"When you care about what you do, you do it. But someday your job could be replaced or you will leave the company to do something else. And five years from now, no one will remember that you were the one that developed the system that doubled efficiency results, but your kid will know that you cared. I am replaceable at work; I'm not replaceable at home. At any one moment, I am sacrificing one for another."*

Lisa recommends that women make their work worth it. *"Take a moment and look at everything you are involved in and decide what you want to be good at and do that—or you can be viewed as a failure if you try to do it all." "Sometimes you just have to say 'this isn't for me' and walk away; sometimes you make the choices that sacrifice one thing over another."*

Lisa recommends that you make the choices that serve you best. Sometimes that means doing the added work for your company sometimes it does mean you are not available because you are at your son's game. Keep in mind that whatever you choose, choose it without regret and honor your choice.

"Sometimes it just has to be about me." Lisa says with a smile.

In an interview with John Bussey for his article "How Women Can Get Ahead" (*The Wall Street Journal,* May 2012), Angela Braly, CEO of Wellpoint, shared, *"The myth is that women and their families don't have to make tradeoffs to have an 'extreme career'; they absolutely do. How you prioritize your life and career is your choice. Once you have made a decision, stick to it, don't always second-guess yourself."*

As women we are faced with so many more choices: career, home life, men, children or not; caring for a dog or even a plant could be a challenge.

Only you can choose which choices work best for you. And they may change from time to time, and that's okay too.

You probably have systems for your organization. So how can you systemize and streamline your life? Start by identifying the most annoying time-waster you choose to engage in. What can you give up?

I have to admit that in my house, I have a sign that says "I kiss better than I cook," because cooking is not my "thing." I do manage to do it anyway. Some time ago I was grocery shopping with my son when he was a young teen. He demanded to know my plan for every meal of the week. I know I turned heads when I muttered aloud, "Just because I was born with breasts doesn't mean I had to feed people all of my life." To me, grocery shopping and getting my nails done (necessary) are a waste of time. I hate being locked down with the cart (an easy task to off-load) or under the nail dryer (not so easy to off-load—they're my nails!) unable to move, to work, to communicate, to do what I do best.

Women who succeed get the help that they need when they need it. Hiring the 12-year-old down the street to wrap the more-than-100 Christmas gifts we give was my greatest gift to myself. She was happy to earn an above-babysitting rate while watching TV from the dining room table. My gifts looked spectacular with special ribbons and bows tied lovingly by her calm hands.

I've found that giving tasks to other people allows them to do what they feel brilliant at so I can do what I do best.

So, what can you off-load to give freedom to your brilliance?

Remember: It's your life, so you get to choose. Why not choose *not* to do it all?

HOW ARIANNA HUFFINGTON STOOD TALL—BY LYING DOWN

When it comes to living the kind of life that would mark one as a "good person," there are many euphemisms, colloquialisms, and figures of speech that try to capture the method you should take to achieve that goal. "Stand tall." "Be the bigger person." "Rise above the pettiness and drama." As it turns out, those figures of speech are not all that far from the literal sense of the word. Being the bigger person really does sometimes mean being the bigger person.

But in a world where corporate scandals and business closings seem to be a dime a dozen, some might say that concept has been lost. Can you succeed while being the bigger person? Or at least by being true to who you are without apology? There is a large body of evidence that suggests that this would be an area where women have the advantage. Research today shows that in areas where social and emotional skills are required in business, women are leading the pack.

What does this mean? That women may, in fact, rise above their male peers in the corporate world in the future by simply being better at "rising above." Arianna Huffington sees the world moving exactly this way, and her Pulitzer Prize–winning media dynasty is just one example of how the cream rises to the top when you don't sacrifice your principles.

How did she do it? She did it by lying down.

Before 2007, Arianna Huffington was just another CEO wanting to have it all, balance it all, and be able to stay awake the entire time while she did so. She would spend hours every single day creating what you may read every morning, *The Huffington Post*, while driving her daughter around America to visit colleges. In order to make up for lost business time, she would clock long hours at the computer when she got home from the road. One day it caught up with her, and she fainted at her desk.

She didn't just faint. Her head hit the desk and, five stitches and a broken cheekbone later, Arianna knew she needed to make some changes.

She settled a little wrinkle with AOL to the tune of $315 million in 2011. She also wrote an op-ed for the *Wall Street Journal* in response to *Lean In*, suggesting that women shouldn't just do that—they should also do something else: lean back. And relax a little bit. And focus on the core values that make you a woman, and don't apologize for that.

Huffington also extolled the virtues of women who know how to take care of themselves. And after her scare in 2007, she wasn't going to let that happen to her, or any of her employees, again.

"Stress less, live more" became her choice—and she won't say a single sorry about it. She now oversees more than 200 employees, and it is her personal mission to make sure they are each taken care of before the paper goes to bed. In fact, if her staffers haven't slept first, the paper doesn't go to bed, either. To make sure her ship runs smoothly, she provides just that for them. Each of her offices now houses office nap rooms, meditation centers, and in some even a yoga room.

She says, *"We're a 24-hour newsroom. We pride ourselves on being first. It's just as important for each of them to be healthy as it is for me to be healthy. Wellness is paramount to the success of Huffington Post."*

Today, Arianna Huffington has a net worth in excess of $35 million dollars. She may have even gotten some of that while she was napping. And she doesn't apologize for staying true to who she is.

Women are simply better at taking care of each other. We are also just better at being nice in all areas of life. Time spent trying to hide that is time wasted and could also mean losses for your business. Those qualities will only work against you when you apologize for having them. Instead, follow Arianna Huffington's lead and lean back. Then, stand tall and allow that part of you to shine and work for you. The end result? Rise above, by rising above.

HEEL PRINTS: HOW TO PUT A DENT IN THE UNIVERSE, ONE WELL-HEELED STEP AT A TIME

9

Meet Heidi Copeland,
CEO, Millyard Communications

Heidi always had a passion for journalism, and at a young age became the first woman publisher in Boston, Massachusetts. An innovative Renegade Leader in heels, in 2010 she followed her dream and became the proud owner of the publishing company Millyard Communications, Inc.

Her advice to women is to be as fluid and flexible as her personal passion, dancing. *"It's all about getting your heels on and being enthusiastic about what you do, and less about precise footwork. You just have to go out there and have a good time."*

"In business a leader needs to be confident, like a good dance partner who knows how to lead so that employees will trustingly follow. They need to feel that you are in charge and you know where they are going."

"Journalism is a great career for women. "The field is fabulous. It used to be predominately male, but recently more women have snapped up opportunities." Just be passionate about what you choose. *"The luxury of success is that you can pursue things that are fun."*

Success isn't always immediate. *"Tripping on your own shoes is all part of learning the dance steps." Separate your life from work. Take the time to dance, to go to your exercise class, to follow your passion wherever your steps take you. When more humanity enters the workplace, everyone will be happy and much more productive."*

For Heidi, her heels are happy to hit the dance floor.

Heidi's advice: *"compartmentalize your work—to separate your personal and professional lives—but the key is to make sure to live both fully."*

So much has been written about balance; these gifted women who opened their doors, their hearts, and their lives to share with you make the choices that suit them best each and every day. Determine your choices by knowing what is important to you and your future ... the legacy you wanted to leave behind

In my second master's degree program, the professor asked us what we wanted written on our tombstone. Many classmates said "best mother, wife, sister," etc. Without thinking I said, "She was the light that ignited others." Being the light that brings out the radiance in others is what I do; it is part of who I am so that commitment dictates how I do my work and how I relate to those around me. It guides my every decision.

What heel prints will you leave behind in the world? The choices are endless. What can you as a leader of self, others, or an organization do to empower others—to make your mark on the world and leave your heel print behind? Let's see what the women I interviewed are leaving behind.

LEAVE YOUR WORLD BETTER
THAN YOU FOUND IT

Kathy Eberwein leaves her mark wherever her companies go, selecting an initiative designed to benefit every location they are in, including funding programs to reduce disease in Africa, taking on the cause of sex trafficking in Asia, and supporting breast cancer research, to name just a few.

LIFT AS YOU CLIMB

Leesa Smith has a passion for inviting women leaders into leadership, overseeing a women's leadership program and a diversity program while also donating her time to sit on the Red Cross board.

Women often lack the networking systems our male counterparts have taken for granted for generations, so it's important to develop a way to support all the leaders in-house. Encourage those around you to show their brilliance. Hold up a mirror and show them their capabilities—even if they don't see them for themselves.

PLANNING YOUR NEXT 40 YEARS BASED
ON THE CULTURE YOU CREATE TODAY

Wendy Tirollo takes the time to schedule a company picnic while still meeting deadlines, walking the halls of every department, and asking her staff, "Do you have what you need? How can I help you?"

CLICKING HEELS IN SUPPORT OF BUSINESS

Heidi Copeland and Robin Comstock support the dreams of businesses by giving them the support they need to be seen as leaders in their industry. They champion businesses to their greatest level of success, make connections, and highlight the wins and advancement of the leaders they meet.

CHANGING AN INDUSTRY—ONE HEEL PRINT AT A TIME

Jo Ellen Nash offers her unique footprint by giving her business clients an experience that they typically don't find in her industry and commits herself to helping others to achieve excellence.

SHARE YOUR SUCCESS WITH OTHERS

With Lisa Allen's careful financial measures and oversight, her company shares their growth and profitability by serving the community. It's given over a million dollars to serve those in need. Her company recently launched its non-profit organization, FEEDNH, so they can give back to the community and have even great impact. Corporate dedication has had a pay-it-forward effect: Teams of employees are now adopting and supporting the causes that resonate with them.

OPEN THE GATE TO OTHER POWER SHOE WEARERS

You can instill opportunities for mentoring for leaders, men and women alike, to benefit.

In summary, whether you reach hundreds of people or just a few, the heel prints you leave behind can be the most rewarding aspect of your work. Some dents will be smaller than others, but when even one life is changed, no dent in this universe is too small. The beautiful thing is that we all have the opportunity to create the legacy we leave. What will be yours?

CONCLUSION
MOVING FORWARD:
STRIDES FOR SUCCESS

As I mentioned at the beginning of this book, Marilyn Monroe said, "Give a girl the right shoes and she can conquer the world." We all know when it is our time to step into our power shoes.

My life changed when I slid into my heels on those steps of Bankers Trust that day in New York City. It's impossible to curl up small or lean forward or backward on heels without falling over. Without them I might have given into the fear, the trepidation I felt, the fear of being inadequate. At that time, I didn't understand the rules of engagement of business or the language of leaders, calling on the executive giants on the top floors of Fortune companies. I subjected myself to constant self-scrutiny, asking, "Am I enough? Do I belong here?"

Yet failure was never a choice. And isn't that how it is when you choose to step forward?

The click of the heels across the marble lobby floor reminded me of the importance of the work that I had to do. Knowing it wasn't about me. It was about providing technology solutions that would bring a company together, that would connect all of their people, their processes, their procedures, and their communication. It would build a culture of high performance and profitability, and promote a culture of positivity.

Connection always does.

To finish the story, I soon made that first sale to Bankers Trust, and a list of Fortune 500 clients soon followed in New York City and later in Boston. Using my natural curiosity, my heart-centered empathy, and the innate skill of collaboration to build consensus, I deepened my relationships with my current and perspective clients and my team.

As a result I was able to uproot my incumbent competitors, surpass the results of my male colleagues, and catch the eye of my corporate leaders. I became recognized as one of the nation's top sales performers and was later promoted to national account manager, overseeing the team of engineers, trainers, and technicians that implemented the services of the $8 million installation I gained that required implementation in 30-plus countries for my client, a global defense contractor.

I now realize what led to my success then and continues to contribute to the success I bring to my clients now. It's the same success you bring to your organization as a leader.

Leadership is about building relationships and gaining consensus. Self-leadership means having a deeper relationship with yourself in the context of your goals and desires. To walk unapologetically and confident in who you are. Leading others begins with launching personal relationships—developing those strong connections that women are naturally able to forge so that you can effectively lead your team, manage conflict, and deal with performance challenges. Leading an organization widens the scope of your relationships, expanding outward to include your customers, stakeholders, industry, and the legacy you will leave behind.

All of these positions allow you to give way to your innate strength as a woman.

When I entered corporate the suits I was wore came with shoulder pads. But those suits didn't fit our round bodies, and our slender arches weren't suitable for narrow wing tips.

> "Remember that you can do anything you want to do. Don't let anyone say, 'You're not smart enough...it's too hard...it's a dumb idea...no one has done that before...girls don't do that.' My mom gave me that advice in 1973. And it allowed me to never worry about what others were saying about my career direction."
>
> ~ Meg Whitman, President and CEO, Hewlett Packard

The old way doesn't fit, for men or women, but for the first time in history there is an opportunity for you to take the lead and still embrace your femininity. Just as I stood tall on those steps in New York City, I stand committed now to create a shift in leadership. I coach men how to shed the exterior most of them are tired of wearing and to promote a more engaging style of leadership at all levels, not just from the top down. I coach women leaders to embrace their authenticity to become leaders others will want to follow, I show them how to leverage their femininity, and I give them the specific tools and support they need to break through performance and profit barriers so they can successfully expand their influence.

As mentioned, my clients have been able to grow award-winning companies, increase their profits many-fold, and receive national awards and recognition for their leadership roles, all while enjoying their own authentic version of success.

But in order to advance, you have to step forward.

I do believe it is about the shoes—the shoes that keep you on the move, the mindset that keeps you driven, and the passion that will fuel the flame of your capability. But with all of the work of leadership, hurdling over the obstacles in your path, or simply the loneliness at the top, it is easy to lose sight of the magnitude of your potential—the possibilities that lie ahead.

But the good news is that you don't have to do it alone. Imagine surrounding yourself with people who challenge you to step forward, who stabilize you when you are wobbly on your heels, and who cheer you on as you advance.

That is why I established a place where you can join a community of other, like-minded women for whom success is the only option. It is a place where you can try out new ideas, express yourself fully, and network to get the resources you need.

Sometimes you need to line your shelves with shoes that are not your own to enrich the fullness of your closet, to add diverse perspectives to your vision, and to bring color and laughter to your world. Think of it as your local café to gather in conversation, your leadership university portal, your coaching corner, and your mentorship.

You've learned about the soul-less state of leadership today; with business and employee engagement results slipping further and further, it is easy to see what is not working.

A new paradigm is needed—a breakthrough, a Renegade way where all leaders shed their traditional skins and trade them in for their Renegade entrepreneurial spirit and people-centered skills—so we can focus on what is possible.

Women will lead the new economy. You have what fits, and with empathy, collaboration, communication, and engagement in your DNA, you are bound to succeed.

The studies show us what we need to do. The L.E.A.D. Forward Formula™ offers a blueprint for how to do it, how to promote self-leadership, how to engage your teams, and how to build the culture of sustainability. Profits are created by happy people; positive workplaces and profitable, sustainable businesses give back in the world, creating a vaster ripple of influence.

Since what we have isn't working now, I feel we don't have any other choice.

But not everyone steps forward. Will you?

We do tend to stay safe when we are alone; it is the collective intelligence of those around us who challenge us to be our best—who push us to take risks, to move out of our comfort zone, and to wear the shoes that seemed only meant for others, until we can call them our own.

People are waiting for you to show up—to do the work you were meant to do. I'm inviting you to come up above the radar. To be unapologetic about who you are. To live life fully in your purpose and passion shoes.

It's time to pack your bags and change your mental zip code to a neighborhood that best serves you. To uproot any of the lies you've been told or are telling yourself, and get to know your truth. To shine the light on the shadow of any fear you've been standing in and trust that that light will guide you on your path to success.

If you've ever found yourself playing a smaller game than you are capable of, I'm here to tell you it's time to play full out. If you are waiting for your permission slip, consider it written.

If you've ever had dreams that haven't materialized, I'm here to wake you up so you can take the actions you need to succeed; and if you are on the bottom of your own to-do list, I'm here to bring you to the top. The first move is yours; it's your choice to stay in the shadow of your vast potential or to step forward with conviction into what you know to be true, claiming the space only you can own.

I'm going to extend an invitation to you to stand up, take that first step, and join other heel-wearers to do the work and to take the actions. And I've established a community to support you.

My clients live on the edge of the box. They set upright what has fallen down. They impact the world, set the standard for others, know and tell their story, get seen, are heard, and turn heads to get noticed. They have a voice, they see things in a different perspective than most, and they are here to live an amazing life and to leave significant heel prints behind. I want you have this too.

When Sarah Palin gave her speech accepting the vice presidential nomination at the 2008 Republican National Convention, she asked, *"You know what the difference is between a hockey mom and a pit bull?"* The answer, of course, was "lipstick."

I say it is heels, those shoes that elevate you above the crowd and prepare you to take those forward steps.

Palin went on to say, *"Life is too short to compromise time and resources.... It may be tempting and more comfortable to just keep your head down, plod along, and appease those who demand: 'Sit down and shut up,' but that's the worthless, easy path; that's a quitter's way out. And a problem in our country today is apathy. It would be apathetic to just hunker down and go with the flow. Nah, only dead fish go with the flow."*

I wrote *Running in High Heels* to help you to elevate your success, to make sure your message is heard, to discover your brilliance, and to illuminate your bright light so the world turns and notices you.

Now, you have the behind-the-scenes strategies to:

- Break free of the status quo and to turn your ideas into edgy, actionable leadership strategies.

- Stand out in today's modern economy while working more effectively, not harder.

- Show up unapologetically to create an authentic and powerful presence.

- Use your own power voice so your message will be heard and acted upon.

- Create a company culture of positivity to maximize performance and profitability.

- Leave a unique, authentic, and impactful legacy.

- Be comfortable in your own shoes while doing it.

Of course, you can take all of the suggestions in this book and take those first steps on your own. But wouldn't it be more fun to team up and walk with other heel-wearers like you? I think that, as women, we're stronger together. So, simply because you've read *Running in High Heels,* I'm offering you an invitation to drop into our virtual community—to stop in, say hello, look around, and collect what you need in resources. And to meet other women who, like you, are ready to step up and change their lives, their workplaces, and maybe the world.

Collect your free stuff!

Visit http://www.therenegadeleader.com/BookResources to gain exclusive entry to self-assessments, current articles, and other materials to support you, your teams, and your organization. Consider it a "gift with purchase."

I look forward to seeing you on the leadership runway!

WEB-BASED RESOURCES:
GET YOUR FREE STUFF!

- ➢ Guest passes to leadership webinars and events
- ➢ Checklists
- ➢ Articles
- ➢ Interviews
- ➢ Access to our exclusive leadership portal
- ➢ Monthly *Insights for Influence and Impact* tip sheets
- ➢ Self-assessments

And so much more!

Go now to http://www.therenegadeleader.com/BookResources

TAKING IT FURTHER...
HOW TO TURN INFORMATION
INTO TRANSFORMATION

Want the Running in High Heels Experience?

WHAT'S POSSIBLE WHEN YOU
L.E.A.D. FORWARD?

Imagine a company culture in which the positive energy is palpable. Imagine your team working together to share ideas and synergy and creating new solutions and paths toward successful outcomes. Imagine leading a team that embraces change. Picture an environment where success is contagious and everyone is committed to a shared vision—your vision.

Now imagine this is your *company*—your *team.*

The effects of people-centered leadership on a company's bottom line are astounding. Performance isn't the only thing that soars; profits also soar. With increased engagement, teams function better, tasks are performed with ease, little time is wasted, and there is greater commitment to improving the bottom line in all areas. Engaged employees perform 30% more than disengaged, and 87 percent of them remain loyal to their company. Engaged employees arrive committed to their work and are aligned with the shared values of the organization. As a matter of fact, 68 percent want a stake in reducing costs and improving the bottom line, and 72% of engaged employees believe they impact service delivery and client retention.

As countless studies have already determined, what worked in the past no longer works today—and too many organizations are stalled as a result. It's our passion to help leaders to move forward and to build thriving cultures.

As a leader you can step in and activate what is needed for modern business to succeed.

At the Renegade Leader Coaching and Consulting Group, we have worked with leaders for more than two decades to increase the performance and growth of their companies, and expand profits and market share, all while creating great places to work. We constantly research what is needed to help you be successful in today's market, survive long-term economic changes, and stay adaptable in a world of steady change. I hope *Running in High Heels* has given you some ideas to get started.

Now that you've learned an overview of the L.E.A.D Forward Formula™ are you ready to evolve not only to the style of leadership that is effective for today's workforce but to ignite your renegade spirit, step forward and realize your full potential?

During my years as an executive coach, I have worked with hundreds of women Renegade Leaders who have distinguished themselves and their organizations from the crowd, all while enjoying their own authentic version of success—a version that also gives them time to enjoy the rewards of that success with friends and family.

I also worked with smart men—men who were open to hearing about how putting people before profits would expand their organization, and lead to growth, sustainability, and—yes! —higher profits.

It all begins with making a choice to lead and claim your place as an innovative leader who can reimagine, rethink, and reinvent what's possible and have the courage to act upon it.

You've learned about the CEOs who have created and manage powerful businesses because they had the vision to succeed. However, we can't do our work alone. Robin Comstock said that you are not a leader unless you have hands to hold you. You need to align others to your vision. You can align them by painting the vision brightly, communicating it clearly and creating a culture that will support its success.

It's one thing to know what to do, another to do it.

For emerging and front line leaders in our Leadership Academy for Renegade Leaders we tell participants that they have three actions 1) Make a choice, choose who you are as a leader 2) Gain the skills you need to succeed and 3) Have the courage to use the skills to lead forward. You might be a leader who works in traditional environments where innovation and thinking outside the box are discouraged. You might want you discover ways to reignite your Renegade spirit to find expression before its fire goes out. Coaching gives you the skills and the mindset – to step into your Renegade roles and lead with gravity defying confidence.

For the executive business leaders we work with work with, we co-create the relevant solutions that meet your company's unique needs, working across many divisions of a company to carry a consistent message forward. We provide proven and innovative strategies to mobilize employees, have more influence, lead change, create an engaged culture, increase revenues, reduce costs and jumpstart innovation.

It is easy to have a vision, harder to pass through the door of what it takes to achieve it.

Unless you are a Renegade Leader.

My Commitment

I'm here to bridge the gap between the leader who is stuck in the paradigm of old structures that no longer work to the modern Renegade who leads with innovation, impact, and unstoppable confidence.

When a Renegade leader steps into his or her fullest potential, they light the path for other leaders to do the same. The leader benefits, the employees benefit, and in the end, the company benefits. It's my greatest joy to make this happen one leader one organization at a time.

It's time for a change and I'm stepping forward to do it. I am closing the gap, creating the much needed shift in business and leadership for business to survive in the modern economy.

Are you willing to join the journey?

Why not make the choices top leaders are making to grow their businesses, evolve as Renegade Leaders and to pioneer a new path in business where no competitor yet exists?

If you are curious how to get started, let's have a conversation and I promise you will leave with an immediate action you can take on the path of a Renegade Leader.

Are you Ready to Activate the Renegade Leader Within?

Conversations with the Author:

Contact The Renegade Leader Coaching & Consulting Group at:

603-324-7171 or 800-891-6875 or complete
our Contact Us application at

http://www.TheRenegadeLeader.com

**Consider this your personal invitation to leave behind
every compromise and step into what is possible.**

ACKNOWLEDGMENTS

I've always been a lifelong learner, excited by the latest research studies, interested in evolving business trends, intrigued by the study of psychology, neuroscience, and human dynamics, and always open to the endless well of information. My friends believe that having a total of 19 letters after my name should be enough—but I am far from done learning. I am grateful to those who have supported me and my work, and served to saturate my endless thirst for more.

First I'd like to thank the pioneers in leadership who formed the foundation from which to build: John C. Maxwell, Daniel Goldman, the late Stephen R. Covey, David Logan, and John King, who introduced the concept of tribal teams; Jim Collins, who tracks what makes organizations great, what builds them up, and what makes them fall; Steven Pressfield, who encourages us to Turn Pro in all that we do; Deborah Tannen for identifying the gender gap in communication and Suzanne Bates who takes this further; Lisa Nichols, who taught me how to "show them" versus "tell them" and who created a movement despite being told she couldn't and for those who are taking a stand, telling their story, and encouraging women to do the same; Tamara Mellon, co-founder of Jimmy Choo; and Sheryl Sandberg of Facebook. I also thank the innovators of our time such as David Rock, founder of the Neuroleadership Institute, for providing the education that keeps me and my clients on the leading edge of understanding people, motivation, and leadership, and for pointing out where psychology and business intersect. Special thanks to Andrew Neitlich, founder of the Center for Executive Coaching.

Thank you to the women CEOs who invited me into their offices and into their business worlds to listen and give print to their advice and the sparkling gems of wisdom they learned along the way. These experiences not only provide a benefit to the reader but served as a reminder to myself to think bigger, to take action on the goals that scare me the most, and to serve in the greatest capacity so I, too, leave my heel print behind.

Through these interviews I learned how valuable connection, mentorship, and having access to current research would benefit the leadership and committed myself to providing both a web base of resources beyond this book as well as community where leaders can support one another.

I thank all of the mentors I've had along the way: Susan Harrow and Alison Luterman for narrowing my speech to media-ready sound bites; Heather Produska, who helped me define my own clear voice brand and get my message out into the world; Jennifer Kemm, who confirmed the archetype of my brand; Kendall Summerhawk for her endless gifts of knowledge, clarity, and inspired action; Donna Kozik and her team for inspiring me to continue to write, even when it was painful, Melissa Evans for reminding me to stand strong in spirit; and for Lisa Sasevich— admiring your climb to the Inc. 500 is inspiring women to do the same.

Special thanks to those closest to me: my sister, Pat Pappal, who for years has served as best friend, fellow concert goer, and wise one; Susan Hayward, who keeps me energized and centered while she serves as a guru on the mountain and travels worldwide, taking my best little black dress with her; and to those who walk with me on their own personal and professional adventures, Patti Woodson, Barbara Trautlein, and Keiko Hsu.

Lastly I thank my clients: It is for you that I leap out of bed in the morning, excited to share your journey; and my editor, Lisa Canfield, for her quick wit and endless humor. Her expert editing gave structure to the book yet preserved its voice, tone, and Renegade spirit.

ABOUT THE AUTHOR

Debora J. McLaughlin, internationally certified executive coach, leadership expert, and APA Board-certified psychotherapist, uniquely combines 25 years of real-world experience in corporate sales, consulting, public relations, coaching, psychology, and neuroscience with certifications in multicultural diversity, executive coaching, and business coaching to empower leaders to achieve transformational personal and professional goals.

As CEO of the Renegade Leader Coaching and Consulting Group, she works with executives, CEOs, and business owners to maximize their leadership success, create high-performing teams, grow business, and increase profits through executive coaching, assessments, leadership development, business coaching, and organizational consulting.

Known for her keen ability to crack the code on human dynamics, Debora enables leaders to get the results they desire by inoculating organizations against distrust, fear, lack of accountability, and disorganization. Instead she builds collaborative cultures of engaged, energized, and spirited employees led by confident, innovative leaders. Her dynamic personality and willingness to share the truth makes her a valued mentor, giving the bright leaders she works with the specific tools and supports they need to succeed. As a result, many of her clients have been able to grow award-winning companies, increase their profits many-fold, and receive national awards and recognition for their leadership roles.

Debora is best-selling author of *The Renegade Leader: 9 Success Strategies Driven Leaders Use to Influence People, Ignite Performance and Impact Profits*, and co-author of *Blueprint for Success: Proven Strategies for Success and Survival* with Stephen M.R. Covey and Ken Blanchard, and *The Roadmap for Career Success* with Lisa Martelli. She was also featured as one of Corporate America's 10 most-requested speakers and trainers in *Straight Talk for Getting Results* and is one of the nation's top coaching experts featured in *No Winner Ever Got There Without a Coach*.

Her clients include Fortune 500 companies, privately owned businesses, non-profits, and driven leaders from companies such as Bankers Trust, Arthur D. Little, Southern New Hampshire Hospital, Boston Scientific, State Street Bank, Homeland Security, Krupp Companies, Thomson and Thomson, Grinnel Corporation, EG&G, Easter Seals, and Great NH Restaurants, to name a few.

Debora's penetrating conversations are found in media such as *Leadership Excellence* magazine, *Yahoo Finance, IT Business Net*, American Management Association, CBS *Money Watch, Boston Herald*, and Sirius Radio, and she is a frequent guest panelist on international telesummits.

She has received multiple awards for business and executive coaching, and was the recipient of the 2013 Women of the Year Award by the National Association for Professional Women. She holds two masters degrees from Hunter College and Rivier University, holds multiple coach certifications, and serves as board member for FEEDNH.

Contact Us:

The Renegade Leader Coaching and Consulting Group
One Tara Blvd, Suite 200
Nashua, NH 03062
800-891-6875
603-324-7171
www.TheRenegadeLeader.com

MORE THAN A LEADER...

In today' business world it's not enough to be a leader.

Not enough to be successful.

It takes something more.

More than education, more than experience.

It takes courage.

Confidence.

To have vision to look forward.

To be willing to reinvent, reimagine, and rethink what's possible.

To see opportunities where others see challenges.

To unlearn what you were taught and go with what you know.

To leave behind every compromise and have the courage to act.

And to get the tools and skills you need to succeed.

The time is now.

Businesses are closing, people are disengaged, and profits are diminished by lack of passion.

It's time to step forward—to step up.

To take the lead in ways others can't envision.

To distinguish your business from the rest.

To make the choice.

To choose the type of leader you want to be.

You can be ordinary or you can be extraordinary.

Walk in the shoes of a Renegade Leader and lead forward.

~ Debora McLaughlin

INDEX